BATTLE READY

BATTLE READY

OLLIE OLLERTON

BLINK
bringing you closer

Published by Blink Publishing
80–1 Wimpole Street,
London,
W1G 9RE

facebook.com/blinkpublishing
twitter.com/blinkpublishing

Hardback – 9781788703369
Trade Paperback – 9781788703376
Ebook – 9781788703390

A CIP catalogue of this book is available from the British Library.

Designed and set by seagulls.net
Printed and bound by Clays Ltd, Elcograf S.p.A

1 3 5 7 9 10 8 6 4 2

Blink Publishing is an imprint of Bonnier Books UK
www.bonnierbooks.co.uk

This book is dedicated to every person that reads these pages. To all that have dreamed big and failed, to all that fall foul to procrastination and hesitation and to those that have lost their way.

To every living soul that strives for greatness and feels uneasy in this modern world, constantly repeating cycles that make no sense at all.

This book serves as a guide to put all that read its words back on track, focused and proud of who they are.

Surrender to yourself and fortune will prevail.

'Nothing in life was ever great, unless at some point you doubted your ability to achieve it.'

Ollie Ollerton

CONTENTS

THE PROMISE

I _____ ,

on this day, state my intention to achieve

_____

_____

_____

and give my personal promise to follow the programme I have designed for myself. For the duration of the programme I will remain focused and disciplined, implementing and executing all my designs to the best of my ability. I will become Battle Ready.

Signed

_____

(See page 202 for more information on making a contract with yourself.)

PROLOGUE

It's a scorcher of a summer's day and me, my brother Justin and mate James are wandering into town to the baths to cool down. It's the eighties, we don't have computer games that are worth staying inside for, our domain is the outdoors. As we cross a bridge over the River Trent, the air is buzzing with dragonflies. As we watch them skimming like Hueys over the water, we notice a circus being set up on a patch of nearby wasteland; a huge Big Top being hauled into the sky, its striped canvas skin flapping like ships' sails among the rigging of cables. We walk around the brightly coloured tents, their guy ropes taut with pegs hammered into the dry summer grass. I smell candyfloss and diesel in the breezeless air and my stomach wheels with excitement. The circus ... there's something electric and dangerous about it. Those apparently *obedient* wild animals can at any moment break their training habits, go feral and turn on the audience, the lions bursting through the pathetic-looking caged barriers hurriedly set up around the stage perimeter.

We hear elephants trumpeting somewhere in the background as we come across an outer circle of caravans and trailers where the performers live, the air now threaded with the aromas of fried onions and hot dogs. Jogging along with excitement, we come across a circus worker with a friendly face by the entrance to the circus and ask if we can have a nose about the animals. The nostalgic glint in his eye, which makes me think he must be remembering his own childhood, says, 'yes' before he's even opened his gob. *Of course you can, lads, and it's rich pickings here for three intrepid, adventure-hungry boys. Roll up, roll up – try your luck on the One-Arm Bandits, test your strength and wield the mighty mallet on the Strongman Game, win a giant cuddly Spiderman toy at the Shooting Gallery, or maybe just go and snoop around the animal cages ...*

He simply says, 'Yes, of course you can. The animals are on chains so don't worry.'

And that's all the encouragement we need as we race off through a labyrinth of grassy pathways between the tents. It's amazing how different our town feels with the arrival of the circus, as if having passed through exotic lands it brings with it some of their magic and the promise of escape. And here's Justin, James and me, three lucky lads being granted a VIP backstage pass.

First up we follow the noise of the elephants, finding them in a large dark tent that whiffs of pissed-on sawdust. The next tent I wander into chatters with mean little monkeys with sharp canine teeth. The little fuckers hiss as I pass by. Entranced by my rare glimpse of this secret other world, I've drifted away from the others and become separated from them. Through a loose flap of the canvas tent whose eyeholes are still to be laced up, I spot something moving in a patch of sunshine outside. Curiosity gets the better of me as I poke my head out in the sunshine like a mole blinking at the light. Jesus, it's hot today!

I wriggle under the canvas into the grassy clearing; it's completely hemmed in by tents and circus vehicles. In this private little oasis spilling with sunshine sits a tiny chimp eating a pile of fruit. He looks like one of the monkeys on the PG Tips adverts on telly where they dress them in human clothes. He glances at me as I stand towering over him, his little brown eyes trusting and innocent, and then he glances back at the fruit between his fingers. He has soft little hands and tiny nails just like a human's, huge comical ears that are translucent pink with brilliant sunshine flooding through them, and his tufty hair is brown one moment then jet-black as he shifts a little from the sun's glare into shadow. It feels as if time has stood still and the Earth has stopped spinning. But for the baby and I looking into one another's eyes, everything else is non-existent.

It feels like such a privilege, I'm completely hypnotised by him. I'll never forget this moment. Then the little fella chuckles, holds out the banana he's been chewing and offers me a bit. I gratefully receive it with a smile and, so as not to upset him, pretend to eat it before discreetly chucking it over my shoulder. This takes things to the next level. Now we are officially friends – Ollie Ollerton, Burton-on-Trent's very own Tarzan, King of the Jungle.

Something shifts in my ten-year-old's peripheral vision, like a black bin bag blown by the breeze. It disappears under the colourful livery of a Foden lorry, reappearing a moment later in a blur of darkness and sunlight. But there *is* no breeze, it's hot enough to fry an egg on the pavement. The bin bag suddenly grows massive arms corded with muscle, and bolts toward me in a weird sideways gallop – a Space Invader covered in fur – and the air is split by a furious, high-pitched scream that cuts through me like someone dragging their fingernails on a blackboard. The beast's coat is so black it appears almost purple in the sunlight, its eyes two points of fire buried in its skull, while its foaming lips peel back to reveal razor-sharp teeth. It crosses my mind that it might be the baby's mother. It also dawns on me I'm frozen with fear and cannot move.

I'm transfixed, the breath captive in my lungs as I watch this terrifying beast hurling toward me, its eyes full of hate. *This can't be happening to me*, I think. Then a moment later something hits me so hard in the sternum that the breath is knocked out of my body, and the ape is on top of me. *Heeeere's Mummy!* It's as if I've picked a fight with the cock of the school five years above me, we're so unfairly matched, the strength in her arms unimaginable. She pounds at me with knuckles hard as rivets, her dense weight pinning me to the spot, jaws wide-open and packed with teeth. I automatically put my forearms over my face to protect it, and between flinging me about like a ragdoll, she expertly goes to work on my body with her canines and molars. I hear bones snapping. As she comes up for breath her teeth are laced with stringy bits of flesh and blood. She's taking chunks out of my arm as if it's a raw bit of steak. I'm being ripped apart. A voice in my heart says, *It doesn't end like this, Ollie.*

Something primal flashes within me like a flicked switch; if there's the smallest chance of survival, I need to fight back while I still have a pair of arms. I either allow myself to die or take a risk and fight back. I have to take this fight to the next level, if there's any chance of me surviving. It's a step into short-term discomfort for long-term gain. It's that simple. The choice is mine. My arms aren't working anymore so I shift my body sideways and unbalance the ape, giving myself a little room to manoeuvre my foot up and smash it into her ribcage. As she falls backwards, I scurry back a few feet. A second later she's flying back at me for the final onslaught. But then, just as the ape is almost upon me, something rudely yanks her back and I realise she has a collar and leash round her neck. I'm just out of harm's way and the chimp is white with rage as she batters the ground, bloody drool and fury flying from her lips. Maybe there is a god? Spent, I lie sprawled and ripped open in the sunlight, my body covered in blood, bits of gristle and white sinew hanging out of my useless arms ... There's no pain, *yet*; I'm deep in shock. Then a circus worker appears and puts her hand to her mouth to stifle a scream.

* * *

The air stewardess tapped me on the shoulder waking me from my nightmare. I shot up in my seat as if I'd been electrocuted, nearly knocking the G&T out of the hand of the passenger next to me. Did I want something to drink? Booze was the last thing on my mind. I'd barely touched a drop in years, while my friend Dave 'Nicko' Nichols had respected the request of the ayahuasca retreat, to which we were heading, and abstained from alcohol for two weeks before our arrival.

As the plane banked, revealing a sea of endless jungle backed by the impossibly blue Pacific, I looked over at Nicko and wondered what the hell we were doing here. We had travelled thousands of miles to Costa Rica in search of a vine dubbed 'the death plant'. The juice of the *ayahuasca* vine is a hallucinogen. Historically, it was used by shamans in the Amazon Basin to treat physical ailments, help mental problems and solve spiritual crises. These days, it's popular among Western travellers looking for personal and vocational insights into their relationships, purpose in life, career choice, and, most importantly for our purposes, it is alleged to help sufferers of PTSD (post-traumatic stress disorder), depression and addiction.

Nicko, an ex-Para and former Special Forces Support Group operative and veteran of the war in Afghanistan, had witnessed his fair share of tragedies during his time there and returned to the UK a troubled man with PTSD. He'd done a spell in jail, was drinking too much and was heading in only one direction.

Being in the Army insulates you with constant process; it gives each day a sense of structure and purpose. Add to that the camaraderie of your fellow soldiers, which creates a bond that is hard to put into words, and you want for little more. But on leaving the Forces, the scaffolding to the day disappears, which can make you easily feel desolate, lost, worthless and forgotten. The contrast couldn't be more acute: in the British Special Forces you are an integral part of the most admired and feared group of elite soldiers in the world; on civvy street you're suddenly a nobody, nothing but a walking mass of scars and trauma. Desperation, anger, fear and emptiness seem to be your only friends. Suicide is a constant siren singing to you from the bottom of a pint. The more you put down your throat, the less clearly you hear her.

Nicko was a walking grenade ready to detonate, and sometimes he did. He'd enter his local and it would go quiet for all the wrong reasons. He looked like someone you wouldn't screw around with, or worse still, like someone who hoped you might. The pub would soon empty, half-drunk pints left standing, while, oblivious, Nicko sat gazing into space with a 'thousand-yard' stare, tumbleweed blowing past his feet. When I was in the Special Forces we dealt with the blackness of war and our operations around the world by matching them with equally dark humour, machismo and aggression. Everyone had the same screwed-up symptoms so none of us realised just how fractured we were. In Afghanistan, Nicko had learned to deal with emotion by deflecting it. The problem was this emotion came back to haunt him tenfold. On leaving the Forces he tried to block it out, didn't share his experiences of conflict, or the loss of his buddies who died in Afghanistan and who he'd never had chance to say goodbye to, with his wife and family. Dave is a big tough lad, a warrior, and as pillars of masculinity warriors aren't supposed to show their weaknesses. And so he tried to bury it. That hadn't worked. Then Nicko attempted suicide, twice: once by hanging, the other time by stabbing himself. Each day was a curse rather than a blessing. He had not only peered over the edge of the abyss, he had fallen to the bottom of it and knew his way around down there. His imminent death sat like a grinning witch's familiar on his shoulder.

I'd given Nicko quite a senior position in my company Break-Point because I believed in him, but there were some staff he'd rubbed up the wrong way who would have been happier to see him go. I felt I had a duty of care, and I honestly think he would have tried to take his life again had I turned my back on him. But for all his complications there was a lot of goodness in him. He had a big heart as well as a great mind, which could be a major feather in Break-Point's cap. We were heading to the jungle in Costa Rica not to take drugs and have a trippy time, but to face our demons.

I'd been intrigued by ayahuasca for some time. Only six months earlier, my old girlfriend Nat, a psychologist who had been doing a lot of work with a hallucinogenic drug called DMT in relation to her treatment of soldiers suffering from PTSD, suggested I would benefit from taking it. As is often the case when you put something out there and focus your attention on an intention, the Universe listens and sends you the coordinates you need to get there. Having expressed an interest in the drug by ticking a page on Instagram, I shortly received a phone call from an American called Jessie. He said he worked for a charity called Heroic Hearts Project, who help military veterans suffering from PTSD by connecting them to ayahuasca therapy retreats around the world. He told me he was in London for a limited time and wondered if we could meet. As it happened, I was in London too, so we got together, talked and he invited me to an upcoming ayahuasca retreat in Costa Rica. My diary was free that week in December and so I was up for it. 'Oh, and did you want to bring a veteran with me?' he asked. I immediately thought of Nicko. The question was, would Dave be open to the drug? I knew the ayahuasca would force him to revisit the traumas responsible for his PTSD. Was there a danger the death plant could tip him into even more mental chaos than he was already burdened with?

Ayahuasca is Quechua for 'vine of the souls'. It's also called the 'truth plant', or 'teacher plant'. They say it takes you to the very core of your real self by confronting you with your self-deceptions, previous wrong-doings, buried trauma and repressed memories. And yet the chance of clearing up old traumas came at a cost. In exchange, we would have to face our deepest fears. A trained spiritual healer, also known as a *curandero* or shaman, would guide us to the black cobwebbed forest of our early memories; a kaleidoscope of bright summer circuses and shifting shadows, nightmares and spiders. It didn't matter how brave I might have been on occasions as a Special Forces soldier, back then I had a team around me. This was something I had to do alone. The shaman would only take me to the woods, he couldn't come in with me and face the horror.

I might have learned to travel light during my time as an elite soldier, but I was still carrying old baggage, the heaviest of which I'd lugged around with me for the best part of my life. And it wasn't just a dream: as a ten-year-old kid, I really was involved in a freakish accident in which a female circus chimpanzee almost killed me. Chimps can weigh as much as 200 pounds, they've been known to kill leopards and, never mind a boy, they are twice as strong as a man. They are also known to eat one another and wage war on rival groups. Human victims of their rage have had their entire faces removed. I began to picture my old foe waiting for me. My whole life had been drawing towards this reunion, that diabolical primate waiting for me upstream in my nightmares, fight-fit and ready. But so was I. I had rebuilt myself bit by bit, both mentally and physically. At 48 years of age, I was finally ready to take it on.

I closed my eyes, relishing the air-conditioned cool of the plane, then started to nod off again. In the dark of my mind something moved, a pelt so black it gleamed almost purple in the half-light, hands leathery and huge as baseball mitts. Statue-still the huge ape waited patiently, eyes fixed on me like amber fires buried deep in the sunken sockets of her face. I fancied I could smell the diesel of circus generators mixed with the tang of animal faeces and candy-floss. Then she opened her mouth, her upper lip peeling back in a hideous grin to reveal yellow incisors sharp as hunting blades, and I almost screamed myself awake. Maybe I wasn't ready after all.

INTRODUCTION

I consider myself lucky and count my blessings every morning and before I go to sleep at night. I have a wonderful woman in my life, a thriving business that I built from scratch with her, a fine son whose friendship is something I cherish, and a black lab called Murphy. But it's not always been hunky dory: if life is a box of chocolates, there have been a fair few razor blades hidden among the orange cremes and strawberry delights I've swallowed on my way here. I've been a delinquent, soldier, Special Forces operative and by turns a drunk and an addict of adrenalin, war, and substance abuse. My highs have often been clouded by dissatisfaction. My lows? Let's just say I could write you a guidebook on how to self-sabotage your life.

In a life spent on the edge of death, be it anaesthetised at the bottom of a bottle or looking down the end of a barrel, I've been the architect of my success as well as my own wrecking ball. And in my obsessive drive to quieten the restlessness that has been an unwelcome spectre throughout my life, I've rattled desperately from one external fix to the next, plastering over the void of emptiness with excessive drinking, adrenalin-seeking in the Special Forces and material acquisition. None of these Band-Aids have worked.

Fortunately, I survived my best efforts to push myself off life's precipice long enough to experience a call to change, a moment of clarity when a voice within me said softly but firmly, 'Enough of this shit! You need to get your life in order. It's now or never.' And at 48 years of age, I can honestly say I'm happier than I've ever been and the reason for this is simple: I found my inner purpose and followed it. Once I discovered it, I nurtured it like I would a precious seedling, and with dogged self-belief and discipline I carefully grew it into my training company, Break-Point, whose MO is to help others. That's my purpose, and I needed to go through the bad shit to find that pearl. A student of life, I'm no intellectual and never went to college, but I love some quotes from thinkers like Nietzsche, the German philosopher, who once said on the subject of purpose: 'A man with a *why* can tolerate almost any *what*.' Without an inner purpose – a why – we're as redundant and unfulfilled as a sailor in a boat with no planned destination.

I reached my lowest ebb when I left the Special Forces and went to work in Iraq, travelling back and forth from my home in Australia. At best I was a functioning alcoholic, earning silly amounts of cash in a war zone, forever haunted by the scars of a broken marriage and guilt-ridden about leaving my son behind. From my first breath to the last sip of booze before passing out most evenings, a death wish was sewn under my skin. At the time I remember saying over and over to myself, 'I don't believe it, how can you have gone from hero to zero so spectacularly? One minute you're an elite soldier, the next you're a failure.' I was running wild without the structure of the SBS to ensure I kept disciplined and operating at a standard of excellence. I had no one that I was accountable to but myself. Without self-discipline you can't achieve anything.

Once you hit rock bottom and decide to stick around, I guess the only way is up. My ascent from the pit of despair didn't happen overnight, and my life today isn't perfect, but looking back over the last ten years at my experiences, the mistakes I made and the steps I took to eventually deal with them, I hope that perhaps some of the lessons I learned might be useful to you.

The start to my recovery might seem like a small step for mankind but it was a massive step for Ollie Ollerton, and that step was getting out of the situation I was in. I devised a holistic programme that governed my mindset, exercise and nutrition. For three months I locked myself away in a Cornish cottage and swallowed books on neurology, philosophy and psychology; positivity, nutrition, anatomy and Ted Talks galore. In the Special Forces you plan everything in minute detail in order to deal with intense crises, and getting myself back on track was the most important crisis I have ever faced. The processes I put together to rebuild myself are the basis of this book, and will, I hope, be of use to you in your life. We all need structures of discipline.

For ease of reference I've divided this book into four parts:

- **The Call to Change** – the moment you decide to do something different
- **Barriers to Change** – likely obstacles that will block your way
- **How to Change** – the techniques I used to get myself out of that pit and start living the life I wanted
- **Sustaining Change** – how you can keep the positivity afloat so it becomes a solid, established part of your being

I spent the early days of my working life in elite military units, surrounded by like-minded positive individuals. When I left the military and over a period of years, that positivity became diluted as I integrated back into society. My thinking and foundation of this book comes from being at the two opposite sides of the spectrum throughout my life, and the ability to analyse everything I think and feel, allowing me to become an emotional observer and not the victim of my thoughts. We are not defined by our thoughts but the actions we choose to execute from our thoughts. It's a choice!

We're not stuck in moulds; we can become whatever we wish. Nobody is forcing us to stick at that job we've been doing for the last ten years and secretly hate. Nor is anybody going to thank us for staying in a loveless marriage that makes us unhappy. Certainly not the other half, they'll silently despise you even more. So many of us are living in unnecessary prisons of our own devising. Russell Brand in his book *Recovery: Freedom from Our Addictions*, paints a vivid picture of modern-day dysfunction:

If you're chugging through life in a job you kind of dislike, a relationship that you're detached from, eating to cope, staring at Facebook, smoking and fruitlessly fantasizing, you can sit glumly on that conveyor belt of unconscious discontent until it deposits you in the grave.

One of the most common regrets from people on their death-beds is that they wish they had taken more risks in life and made those changes their inner spirits were yearning for, but at the time they were too wrapped in fear of the consequence of leaving their comfort zone. Nobody but ourselves constructs those invisible bars and ceilings that limit us. Humans are extraordinary, and when we put our minds to it, we can do amazing things, burning bright trails of benevolence, creativity and generosity. Conversely, we are equally capable of spectacular sloth and a tendency to be sheep, to accept less than we should from our lives and stay where it is safe. To cap it off, we are instinctively prone to negativity, to expect bad things instead of good fortune.

Battle Ready is a war cry against procrastination. It's about you taking control, creating new positive habits, identifying your purpose and setting meaningful goals; building inner resilience, deliberately changing your life for the better, picking yourself up and recovering when things go wrong, and squaring away needless crap that weighs you down – be it debts or outgrown negative self-beliefs – so that you have the mental bandwidth to start realising your passions rather than worrying about stuff that can be sorted out with a bit of focus. If you never find the time to free yourself up, you'll never give yourself a chance to evolve into the person you hoped you would be. It's about acting in the moment of opportunity and allowing momentum and persistence to be the conduit of your every success.

This is a book for all of us who come unstuck and lose our way from time to time, and for those who want to grow into better versions of themselves. I'm going to teach you how I helped myself find what I really needed, how I visualised it and turned it into the life I live today. Humans experience between 70,000 and 100,000 thoughts per day which dictate our emotional state and thus our behaviour. The brain, wondrous a thing as it may be, is eminently lazy. We'll learn about the way it works so we can better understand ourselves, as well as spotting the thinking that holds us back, and identifying how our own ego can get in the way. We need to start looking at ourselves in a different way if we are to be more in the driving seat, becoming our own observer, rather than a puppet yanked by unseen strings.

In the following pages you'll find simple exercises to help you to focus on what you want to achieve, and how to stay positive and get in flow with your real self. The resources to achieve what we wish for are within each and every one of us, but sadly they are sabotaged by a set of ego-driven, socialised behaviours that aren't helpful to us. And then there's our tendency to sleepwalk through ever-repeating cycles and comfort zones, which though familiar are stagnating to future growth. The self-styled techniques in this book saved me from a life of addiction and depression and enabled me to become a contented human being (something I never thought possible) and a successful entrpreneur with multiple businesses. Now it's your turn to try.

– Ollie Ollerton, April 2020

PART 1

THE CALL TO CHANGE

CHAPTER 1

AT THE BOTTOM OF THE WORLD

stood watching the clothes tumble monotonously round and round in the industrial washing machines like sodden corpses. I was working in a gloomy, dingy sweat shop where they washed and pressed laundry en masse for hotels. The pay stank as much as the dirty washing, there was an asbestos roof and many of the sorry souls who punched in and out were struggling single mums. Hanging myself was out of the question – too disturbing for my family to think of me ending my days like that. Slashing my wrists was also out of the question – too much mess for a tidy person like me to leave for others to clear up. No, it would be a warm bath and a load of pills.

'Are you going to do it tonight or just talk about it?' hissed the voice in one ear. 'You'll fuck it up, everything you touch fails … like your attempt at rescuing kids from brothels in Thailand. You're finished, put yourself out of your misery. Then another voice said softly in the other ear, 'That's not how it ends, Ollie. You're going to get yourself together, you're going to run a successful business one day.'

On the face of it, the first voice was more on the money. I was drinking and smoking enough to singlehandedly keep Queensland's alcohol and tobacco industry afloat. And while a part of me continued to believe there was something better waiting for me, I had no idea how I would ever escape the bottomless pit

I'd wound up in. I'd achieved great things before this point, and had a history of success, so the path wasn't completely unfamiliar, I just didn't know how to find my way back to it.

To the outsider, I probably appeared like a sad loner whose face told a story of despair, pickled by booze that I could no longer mask with hilarity. I kept myself to myself, maintained the washing machines with surgical precision, and stared through the paper-thin walls with dead eyes. I was a husk of a man. And if I ever got talking to someone and they enquired about my English accent and wanted to learn more about me, very rarely I might admit I had been in the Marines, but so meekly it was embarrassing and unconvincing. I'd certainly never tell them I used to be a soldier in one of the most respected highly trained fighting forces in military history. They would have looked at me and laughed. And maybe I would have laughed too. Half-heartedly.

This was 2012. To understand how deeply I'd fallen to reach this place I need to give you a bit more context. Let's rewind a few years.

In 2000, I left the British Special Forces, itching to do something different. For all the adventures during my six years with the Special Boat Service, and there were many, I felt unfulfilled, like an actor who has turned up at the wrong job but stays nonetheless and muddles through a part he's not entirely suited to. My behaviour, even by the standards of the maverick regiment, often raised eyebrows, but I was good at my job and so my best attempts between missions to get fired were tolerated. I had a drinking problem to rival Oliver Reed's, but like that old hell-raiser who after a monumental night on the tiles would turn up on set punctual, word perfect, all bright-eyed and bushy-tailed, I too was a successful working alcoholic. After I quit the SBS, and tried a few different jobs in Blighty, I went to work in Iraq as a security consultant. It wasn't just the money that appealed, the main allure was the chance to escape the corrosive relationship with my then wife.

In 2003, I met Nat, a gem of a girl who worked for the firm that employed me in Baghdad. She and I were inseparable from the moment we met at a work's Christmas party in London, and for a time we lived happily together in Chiswick, before relocating to Brisbane in 2004 where Nat became a full-time psychology student. I worked six weeks on and six weeks off, shuttling between a war zone and the comparable peace of Brisbane. But there was a problem: without the close-fitting wetsuit of the SBS to keep me in check with its demands of fitness and exactitude, my drinking had become untenable. I found no real purpose in the security work or anything else. I drank to forget my broken marriage and blanket the guilt of not being the father I'd dreamed of becoming. It was a wrench being away from Luke and not seeing him grow up. So, I binged on a diet of Valium to quieten my escalating panic attacks and drank industrial amounts of booze to take me to the numb place where I could black out. Naturally, Nat eventually had to throw the towel in. Jesus, she was a saint for lasting as long as she had.

Scared of being single and independent, plus the fact I no longer qualified for Australian residency without Nat, I was immediately on the hunt for another girlfriend. I didn't have to wait long. The next day I was invited to a baby shower on the Gold Coast, and two days after a drunken detour I was on my way to San Francisco with my new soon-to-be wife. Her birthday was the same date as mine, it was written in the stars that we should be together. How wrong was I? I knew the marriage was as steady as a house of cards, and that I was taking short-term comfort for what would be long-term pain. And although it was a beautiful ceremony on top of a mountain overlooking the Nevada desert (with not a clichéd Elvis impersonator in sight), even as I stood there at the altar I knew there was only one impersonator present, and that was me. I'd made a very big mistake. By now I was having panic attacks so severe I thought I was dying. And that's when I first thought about intentionally ending it. I'd had a death wish sat on my shoulder for years. Maybe once or twice I'd tried to appease it, pushing the envelope of danger a little too hard. But this was different, it wouldn't be a case of 'Ollie Ollerton, Special Forces soldier died bravely while engaged in a clandestine operation', but by my own hand. Better to leave this life than go insane, which is what I thought was happening to me.

I got back in touch with my ex-girlfriend Nat, who fortunately for me is a psychologist. I told her everything. Nat had no reason to help me, but she was brilliantly supportive and told me, 'Your life is not over, so don't think like that, Ollie. You can change anything you want to, but first you need to put a process in place that's going to get you out of this marriage … for a start get in touch with a lawyer.' I followed her advice and had the marriage annulled. When you're confused, depressed and stressed you don't want to deal with paperwork or a process, you just want to wallow in the depth of your problems. It's so hard to get out of that pit of self-loathing. But Nat helped me figure things out and start to make a plan to move forward. Unless you face whatever it is that's dragging you down and start looking at each of these issues individually, you'll end up with a mind-cocktail of negativity and destruction.

In the interest of losing any sanity that remained in my life, I went back to Iraq for one final job. By the time I eventually left that troubled country in 2008 and tried to settle permanently in Brisbane, I'd been twice divorced and, if it was possible, I had become even more of a wreck. Having briefly got back together with Nat on my return, we soon split and I predictably sought escape in another woman rather than endure the solitude of my own company.

Sarah had received a healthy settlement from her ex-husband and lived in a million-dollar house complete with swimming pool. They might have been palatial surroundings I found myself living in, but I couldn't have chosen a worse place for my mental stability and self-worth if my life had depended on it. Still, I threw everything into this relationship, sold my house and even cashed in my pension to furnish her newly secured million-dollar property. On the surface it was perfect and an off the shelf relationship, but she drank like she had hollow legs and could become the nastiest of drunks, possessing that same easy capacity for cruelty as my first wife. She'd target my vulnerable spots, pouring acid into them with her barbed tongue: What a loser I was … what a bad person for abandoning his son, what kind of a father does that? In many ways she was a female reflection of myself, equally fractured, unpredictable and on a path of self-destruction.

I worked in property for a while and did well at it, but I was soon bored and unfulfilled, and so I quit.

Then, just when I thought it was over, I caught a break out of nowhere. An old mate called Denny who I'd worked with in Iraq and who now lived down the road in Brisbane, introduced me to a guy called Simon. Despite it being a fancy-dress party I recognised him at once; he'd been involved in my Special Forces Selection. Yet another freak coincidence in a life that had been full of them. What were the chances that having last seen him in Hereford I'd now meet him on the bottom of the world?

Simon told me about an organisation he had connections with called The Grey Man. Self-funded and based in Oz their MO was to rescue kids in South-east Asia from being sold to a life in the skin trade. They sent undercover operatives into brothels where they'd identify child prostitutes and either inform the local law enforcement or rescue them personally. Simon wondered if I might like to join them and use my Special Forces skills to train their operatives? While living with Sarah I trained operatives in and around Brisbane and I told them that was the extent of the expertise I was willing to offer. I wasn't prepared to head to Thailand to conduct operations as it sounded so dodgy, with limited or no backup in a country renowned for corruption.

My relationship with Sarah was getting worse and fell apart after an alcohol-fuelled, turbulent night when I decided to make a break for it, seeking refuge at my mate Denny's house, not too far away. It was then I resolved it was all or nothing and decided to head to Thailand to do exactly what I said I wouldn't. But first I would go back to the UK to see my son Luke who I'd not seen for seven years. Seeing Luke was amazing and it was almost like we'd never been apart. He was now a young 11 year-old man and I was so proud to see him. This was so good in so many ways, but also amplified my emotions when it came to what lay ahead.

FALSE DAWN OF HOPE

I loved doing something useful that drew on my past, connecting me to a time in my life when I had enjoyed self-respect. When I'm passionate about something I throw myself into it heart and soul and this was no different. I pledged my expertise and invested my remaining savings from Iraq into the Grey Man, and following a particularly poisonous exchange with Sarah, I told her I was leaving her and hurriedly flew to Bangkok.

The underbelly of Thailand is complex and labyrinthine. It's easy for a Westerner to wade in moralistically against the sex trade, failing to understand that not everybody who offers themselves for sex does so unwillingly. From a transaction of flesh for dollars a working girl is able to send money back to her village on the Laotian border which will feed her grandmother, pay for her little brother's school books, buy food for the buffalo and grains for the family rice padi. Some working girls even use the money to study and eventually leave the skin trade for a better life. But for every story like this there is another of a child barely in puberty being taken from her village, drugged and trafficked to the Golden Triangle, where for the price of $30,000 dollars, tigers, battery-farmed in Laos, can be killed in front of you for your own consumption, balls, teeth and all. A 12-year-old girl from Isaan Province is considerably cheaper. Some girls are sold to Burmese fishermen as a plaything to while away the long hours spent at sea. Used and abused, their torn little bodies are cast overboard into the Bay of Bengal or the Andaman Sea for the fishes to feed on before washing up on the coast as faceless Jane Does.

Helping free these kids from a life in the sex trade filled me with hope and made me realise that helping others was so much more important than focusing on my own woes. Even in the SBS it had been about me and the service, the adventures, the Action Man stuff, were all about me and my ego. But this was different. There was no salary, no plaudits and certainly no backup. We made the decision to work without guns as this might bring assumptions that we were DEA if we were questioned along the way. We were undercover tourists. Our only recompense for the danger we were placing ourselves in was the satisfaction of knowing we were making a difference. If the shit hit the fan and our cover was blown, we had an RV to try and make it to an escape vehicle. One minute I'd be sitting in some dark bar flashing with tired fairy lights, plastic flowers on tin tables, getting loaded on Sang Thip whisky. The next, under the ruse of visiting the bathroom, I'd scope out the layout of the upstairs corridors where the working girls operated in cell-like rooms. Behind their open doors were soiled mattresses on floors, low lights and children with too much make-up on their young faces. The intel we gathered was then used to plan the rescue mission.

I was still drinking an awful lot whenever I got the opportunity of any down time, and even when we were on the job, since that was part of being undercover, getting to know the sex operators and gaining their confidence. But I was on top of it because I felt I was doing something useful, helping people who couldn't fend for themselves.

By the time I had joined them, the organisation had staged an impressive 140 rescue interventions. But sometimes selflessness is closely tailed by pride and having pulled off our biggest coup yet – that of rescuing 22 children in one fell swoop – The Grey Man made the fatal flaw of informing the authorities. The story reached the US State Dept, who annually funded Thailand to the tune of millions of dollars to stamp out the child sex trade, and they erupted with fury. A red-faced Thailand went on the defensive by rubbishing our organisation's credibility, calling us con men and sending their police force to hunt us down. After escaping over the border to Burma we returned with our tails between our legs to Australia.

I was devastated. Not only had I spent all my own money on a cause I believed in, but the chance to help those poor children had been snatched away by the Thai government, and with it the one thing that had so far eluded me all through my life: a true purpose. At my lowest ebb yet, and in perhaps the darkest place I have ever been, against all reason I got back with Sarah.

I tried to keep going, doing a spot of labouring to pay the bills, then working at the laundrette. Every morning I did my best to greet the new day with a sense of optimism, hoping things might change, but that mocking voice – be it my own negativity or Sarah's – took a piss on me and put out any flame of hope.

I was trapped in a toxic relationship I could see no way out of, a vicious repeat cycle mirroring the day before, running on a tread-mill fuelled by self-loathing, comfortable with the discomfort of life.

The downfall of the Grey Man was fresh poison for her to bait me with. If I felt diminished before by her, there's no way to describe the loser I now felt like. Sarah bullied me into getting a nine-to-five job, and I found myself complying by finding employ-ment in a sweat shop laundry. Compared to her mansion of vipers, the place was an escape. Again, I settled into the discomfort of life. A few months down the line, idly loading large sheets into pressing machines, I wondered why I had returned to her and was so scared at the prospect of setting out on my own. It would be hard to start again and rebuild myself but maybe I could fall back on my Special Forces training and start to plan a way back to myself? I had to switch off my emotions first, had to stop thinking of myself and focus on the goal. What was the goal? Mission: Get the Fuck Out.

THE GREAT ESCAPE

By now I had been with Sarah for two years. Two years!? What a waste. It was do or die: if I didn't try another escape, I'd take my own life. I felt like fucking Papillon escaping Devil's Island.

That gentle voice spoke up in my head: 'What's to stop you packing your bag and leaving tonight after your shift here?' I waited for the other voice to counter, the one that liked to piss on me, but there was only silence and the thrum of the washing machine clicking through the next stage of its cycle. In the SBS, we were taught to breathe, recalibrate and deliver; to distance and distract ourselves from the fear curdling in our guts. This was an essential part of training that came in handy when stacking up against a door before entering a firefight. Breathing and recalibrating happens at the same time, lowering the cortisol levels in your brain which make you stressed. I started breathing consciously.

When you're down and out, time becomes immaterial as every day is largely the same, measured by drinks and arguments and night and day are only separated by fresh hangovers and black-outs. Suddenly, life seemed very precious to me; I didn't want to waste any more of it. A flicker of excitement sprang in my chest at the idea of escape. I started imagining myself leaving, my clothes folded neatly in my sports bag, my face clean of stubble and fixed with a determined expression. And, leaving Sarah's forked tongue and insults far behind, I'm running alone like Forrest Gump into my future and a glorious Gold Coast sunrise.

The gum trees outside were turning blue with twilight. Somehow the day had disappeared.

'Well then?' asked the voice gently.

'I can do this,' I told myself. 'I'm ready to change.'

I left Sarah for the final time and took a room in a bright and welcoming three-bedroomed house in Bulimba, on the outskirts of the city. It was too big a leap to immediately live on my own. I was fragile as an eggshell and a hair's breadth from falling back into co-dependency and drink, so I shared with other people. I'm a little OCD about things being tidy but I swallowed the odd cushion being out of place and unwashed plates in the sink in return for the warmth of friendly conversation.

In my little room I felt like I'd escaped from a haunted house.

I had been so far down the well of depression, anaesthetised by a diet of cocaine, Valium and booze, that at times I couldn't string a sentence together, and yet here I was starting out on a fresh path again. And the less I drank, the more that inner critic was kept in the shadows where he belonged. Once you decide to help yourself an amazing thing starts to happen inside you. It's called growth. Every little thing you invest in yourself, from shaving in the morning to eating something healthy, starts to yield more opportunities and insights, and with each of these gifts you become more grateful and positive. You start to notice doors opening. I was drinking less and less and hitting the gym with the energy of a teenager. In recompense for taking the first step, I began to get back some sense of my self-worth and that feeling was addictive.

I lined my energy up with the opportunities in front of me. I'd been for a job interview some time before with an oil company. They stated that I was a little over-qualified for the role, more in respect of the fact they thought I would get bored, which after reading my CV was understandable. But then, out of the blue, they got in touch and wanted me to start as soon as possible. The job offered great pay and a reliable steady income. Maybe somebody up there liked me after all?

EXERCISE: WHAT'S YOUR LIFE LIKE NOW?

Perhaps you haven't reached bottom, like I had in that laundrette in Brisbane. Perhaps your life is ticking along, but deep down you think things could be better. You want your life to change. But before taking that first step, check in with yourself by asking yourself some questions, to give yourself a baseline, a place to start from, and to look back at when you're on your way to achieving your goal. It's good to write these down, and to keep checking in with yourself as you work towards a better future.

DATE: _____

Are you selling yourself short? If so, how?

_____

_____

_____

_____

Are you in a relationship that feeds your confidence or sucks it away?

_____

_____

_____

_____

Do you tell yourself you'll never be a success?

_____

_____

_____

_____

Have you accepted your lot and told yourself not to expect any more from life?

_____

_____

_____

_____

CHAPTER 2

EPIPHANY

You are probably reading this because you want to make a change in your life, and for that I congratulate you: you've bought the right book! It might not be a major change you need, like moving to another country or getting divorced, but it will be something you're not satisfied with. Change doesn't happen overnight; it takes focus and a clear direction of where you want to go and what you wish to change. The first step is committing to that change. This chapter is about identifying *what* you need to change then making deliberate positive steps toward achieving it.

BABY STEPS

As the days in my new Brisbane home went by it was the small steps I took that helped me. Like making my bed in the morning. The first thing you do when you wake up shapes the rest of your day. In his book: *Make Your Bed: Little Things That Can Change Your Life*, retired US Navy Seal, Admiral William H. McRaven says:

> *Making my bed was ... my first task of the day, and doing it right was important. It showed my attention to detail, and at the end of the day it would be a reminder that I had done something well, something to be proud of, no matter how small the task.*

I wanted to be a part of things, among people as it kept me away from solitary thoughts and getting depressed, so I joined the Brisbane Outrigger Canoe Club. This involved being on the water in our canoe by 5 a.m., the sunshine pooling brilliantly on the Brisbane River. I'd then cycle 5km to work, do a training session at lunchtime then cycle 5km back home and then head out in the evening to the Crossfit gym. I was fitter than I'd ever been, fixated on my external image and had pretty much close to 0 per cent body fat. I looked awesome and thrived off the attention my physical image elicited. However, behind this external prowess was someone plagued by insecurity, swollen with ego to be noticed, liked and make new friends. By now my OCD was getting irritated by the other people's mess in our shared house, so I decided to get a flat on my own. I found a place by the Brisbane River, a loft apartment with outside decking and a mezzanine. It was stunning. It was also the first time I had ever spent a night on my own. Ever since being a kid I had always feared being on my own and had been dependent on women. My relationships always overlapped so there was never a chance of my being solo. It was as if I was trading a lease car for a new one. But that first night in the apartment with just my own company was fantastic, so liberating!

I began to reflect on the time I'd lost in my toxic relationship, and that being with Sarah was simply history repeating itself; in that case, my marriage with Helen. Now that I had a job with the oil company, I had a structure within which to reboot myself. As my self-respect returned incrementally, I began to eat healthily, sleep better and exercise, something I had let lapse. I was spending more time outdoors and I even returned to writing poetry and sought out a spiritual psychologist to help me unwrap my troubled past. Since the chimp attack 33 years earlier I couldn't remember any of my childhood. The following poem was written around this time and is about living and not wasting time in fear or anguish. It's also about making the most of your time. Humans are so busy saying: 'When X or Y happens, I'll be content …' but all the while we are wasting the valuable present, which is all we have.

And almost like magic the distance grew into a blur of sound,
And as I looked, I remembered only the recurring memory
Of a time misplaced with fear and anguish!
Who, I asked myself, am I? And as confused as I was
I sat at the pinnacle of something my mind questioned.
Where are you from and why are you here?
I have no fucking idea,
I came here looking for someone I don't want to find,
so lost and desolate I am, why don't you tell me?
Time comes quicker than any moment requested,
if only we could grasp back the moments we would love
    to change!
Your time is yours, what would you do
to make it something you would never forget.

As it turned out, the job with the oil company was a little disappointing due to the lack of structure and decent management, although I was able to carve out some time to focus on myself. As a member of the Brisbane Outrigger Canoe Club, I competed around Australia, winning gold, silver and bronze at several events. I also competed at CrossFit and had an extremely disciplined diet. I was so focused on my aesthetics that I became ripped, but this was a visual distraction for the dis-ease I felt inside. However, as soon as I started mentally investing in myself, I was given a return on my investment. I felt a natural urge to be the positive and spiritual soul that was deep-seated within me. I filled my head with positive affirmations, the most powerful of which was: 'I am ready to accept change, as difficult as it may seem, I know I am being prepared for bigger and better things.'

However, although I was managing to stop drinking in the week, as soon as the opportunity at the weekend arrived, I'd hit the booze big-time like it was some kind of reward. This would sometimes last until Monday, where I would then make excuses I was working from home, and I wouldn't get back on track until Wednesday and then I was back in a repeat cycle of regret and self-loathing. The problem was my job wasn't sufficiently fulfilling. Compared to the work of the Grey Man it all seemed a bit point-less. The frustration of not feeling productive on a professional level was killing me and again I felt like I was heading nowhere and just marking time. For some people the stable job and the security of a good wage was enough, but for me that was the last thing on my priority list.

I devised a technique to start thinking about the things I needed to change. First, I drew a circle with a biro around a CD with dissecting lines through it like the hands of a clock. I wrote my ultimate goal at number 12, and then from 1 to 11 wrote all the steps I had to take to get to that goal. I then focused on where I was and where I wanted to be and wrote that down on every point of the clock. I managed to fill every number from 1 to 12, and had more still to add, but just focused on the dominant 12 problems that were obstructing my path.

For instance, I hated the amount I was still drinking, so in one section I put: 'I am drinking much less' and on the second section I stated: 'I have savings in the bank', on the third: 'I have a loving relationship', and so on, and so on … I then got into the practice of focusing each day on each of the 12 points, and started imag-ining what each of those subjects felt like: I put myself there as if it had happened, and allowed the good feelings of that to dissolve the current and present reality. It's easy to see what my vibration would have been if I had written down everything I hated; it would have amplified my current state and circumstance. I still have the drawing of that first circle and within 12 months of setting the desire and intention, I had achieved each and every one.

EXERCISE: THE CLOCK

Create your own clock. At 12 o'clock write down your ultimate goal and on each hour thereafter (heading clockwise) write down a goal that you will achieve to take you closer to your ultimate goal. This can be a bad habit you have to overcome in order to get to the next step and should be written in the present tense as if you've already achieved it. Create three milestones toward your goal. One at three, six and nine and then as you approach each milestone state the two things you must do to reach that milestone. State them as mantras.

Start with phrases like 'I am …' and 'is …' e.g.: 'I am not drinking', 'My home is clear and clean', 'I am exercising regularly', etc. Date each step, so that you can look back and see how you've progressed.

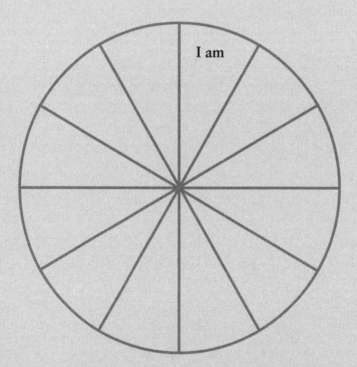

I am

Once you have filled in your clock, put it in a prominent place, so that you see it first thing when you wake up. You might want to make copies and put them around the house – on the fridge, perhaps, or stuck to the bathroom mirror. Starting from the first step, focus on that thought for the whole day. Imagine yourself having fulfilled that goal, what you look like, how you're feeling. The next day, concentrate your energy on step 2, and so on, starting the cycle again when you reach step 1.

Simply by writing your desired changes down you start to breathe life into them. This list of 12 mantras was to start opening doors in my subconscious, and just a few months later I experienced an epiphany that changed my life. It was while I was working for the oil company in Brisbane that I realised I wanted to start my own company. I wanted independence and freedom and something for myself to make into a success. A company might provide me with the sense of purpose I lacked, and some income. The name Break-Point came into my head and I loved it. The name came before the concept of what it represented. At first, I thought it would offer something to do with security, as that was what I'd been doing in Iraq and it felt like a familiar skillset. But it didn't ignite my passion. I found myself unable to infuse my idea with any detail or verve; there was no end goal. But one day, at the oil company, a couple of former fighter pilots came into the office to give us a staff-training day. I thought to myself, 'If they can make this relevant to us, think how useful it would be to teach people skills from the Special Forces … imagine that.' And I did exactly this, I let my mind wander.

A few days later, while on a plane flying across the endless Australian outback, an idea suddenly presented itself to me so clearly I could picture it taking place across the landscape outside my window. I imagined civvies from the corporate sector doing a simulated escape across the outback. I saw veterans suffering from PTSD working as instructors and finding their feet again through teaching mental and fitness techniques to people who wanted to stretch themselves. Break-Point would be an existential rocket up the arse of the beleaguered victims of corporate grind. This was my epiphany, and in that moment all the dots joined together to form a future constellation. It only lasted the blink of an eyelid, that's all you get with an epiphany, but the afterglow on my eyelids left such a strong imprint I knew it was my one and only purpose. If I'd seen a glimmer of it – my desire to help others – in Thailand saving those kids, now it was clear as the sun in a cloudless sky. There was one problem: I just didn't see how I could make it work while having to pay for all these things I'd accumulated whilst living in Australia. Here I was between a rock and a hard place. I'd have to do it in England, and I had vowed never to go back there.

Once I set the desire and started to be so passionate about it, my world in Australia started to fall apart; my contract came to an end and the new contract I was supposed to start was withdrawn, things were not looking great, but what did I expect? I told myself: *You dummy, this is what you subconsciously wanted! And it's not the death but the birth of something. As when something is dying and phasing out it cries the loudest. Be careful not to focus on the tears but pay attention to the serenity of a new life taking shape.*

A few weeks later I bolted upright in bed. It was 3 a.m. on a Thursday. Something inside me said, 'Go home to the UK!' What was I thinking? I promised myself I would never go back but the more I allowed the gate of opportunity to open, the more I could see it all made perfect sense. Within two weeks of this nocturnal thunderbolt I had sold everything I owned on Gumtree and returned to England on 11 July 2014.

CHAPTER 3

FINDING PURPOSE

We are defined by our sense of purpose. When I was in the Special Forces I was an important cog in a well-oiled machine and, although I wasn't entirely satisfied, I felt fulfilled in many ways: the teamwork, camaraderie and sense of a mission provided me with direction. When I left, the gap between myself and my purpose created a monumental void that I failed to understand at the time. It unravelled me very quickly.

Purpose gives meaning to our lives and something to aim for. Those without it get mired in depression and addiction as they attempt to plaster over the emptiness that comes from a lack of purpose. Whenever I've lacked meaning in what I'm doing, my life has spiralled out of control. If you can't think of a purpose, life will find you one, and it will be a lazy choice it makes for you, a safe, grey option the colour of a drizzly Lancashire sky. You'll get sucked in to the false belief that your purpose is to get up at the crack of dawn, spend a big part of your day in transit to work, then do a job whose only function is to pay off the mortgage for a house you barely spend any time in, and you only get to see your kids for an hour in the evening before they have to go to bed. No wonder people end up getting addicted to the first thing that offers them some quick excitement. Without a goal you drift, time passes cruelly by and you can feel utterly pointless. Everyone has a goal whether they like it or not, it is what your dominant thoughts focus on.

The antidote to this is to sit with yourself and really think about how you can find your inner purpose. Your life can be as small or glorious as you allow it but only if you're the conductor, the architect and captain.

Viktor Frankl was a professor of psychiatry and neurology and the founder of a strand of therapy known as logotherapy, whereby patients are guided to find the meaning in their life. His book *Man's Search for Meaning* follows his horrific experience in Auschwitz as a concentration camp inmate. Subjected to freezing weather in poor clothing with no shoes, malnutrition, rats, regular beatings, torture, disease, not to mention the threat of the gas chambers, he lost his wife, mother, father and brother to the camps. Amid all this tragedy and hopelessness, he manged to find meaning in his suffering. He noticed two types of people in the camps: those who had lost all sense of hope and faith, and those who had a *why* to live – something meaningful to be fulfilled by them in the future. This second group saw the daily hell they went through as a challenge to overcome. It was the latter who survived the longest.

So how did he find meaning in his suffering? For Frankl, he found purpose in a manuscript he wished to publish that would help others. He treated all the terrible things he was exposed to as future material for lectures he would one day give on the subject of finding one's inner purpose. Frankl turned a negative into a positive: 'Suffering ceases to be suffering at the moment it finds a meaning.' Frankl believed we need to find meaning in something bigger than ourselves, something outside of us. He also reflected that however much the Nazis tried to dehumanise the Jewish prisoners, they could not take away their right to react to their situation in the way they pleased: they could be reduced to scavenging like dogs or continue to act like humans, practising kindness and attempt to overcome the situation. Your attitude to your existence makes you who you are. He said:

> *Everything can be taken from a man but one thing; the last of the human freedoms, to choose one's attitude in any given set of circumstances ... you and you alone decide what your life will be in the next moment. Man is capable of changing the world and changing himself for the better.*

Frankl also asserts that when we lose ourselves in a task that holds great meaning for us, a cause greater than ourselves, happiness occurs within us as a natural by-product; we shouldn't chase happiness and success per se, but rather dedicate every fibre of ourselves to our purpose and they will both come naturally.

In Okinawa, a Japanese island home to some of the oldest people on earth, the word *ikigai* roughly translates as 'a reason to get up in the morning'. The word derives from *ikuru* – Japanese for 'life', and *kai* meaning 'the realisation of what one hopes for'. In order to find our inner purpose, our *ikigai*, we must ask four questions: What is my passion? What am I good at? What does the world need from me? What can I get paid for?

Answering all four so they complement each other is, according to Okinawans, the path to fulfilment, but it's not always straight-forward. If you're purely focused on earning money but have no passion for what you do, it will leave you feeling empty, while doing what you love but which contributes nothing to the world is selfish and ultimately unfulfilling. When we multi-task naturally our focus becomes diluted. We can only find real flow in ourselves when we cast all our attention on one thing.

I stumbled on the first glimmers of my true purpose, not as a member of the elite SBS but after I left the Forces, when I found myself in South-east Asia, liberating kids from a dark future of prostitution and premature death. My personal balm to a life of empty restlessness, addiction and dissatisfaction turned out to be something as simple as helping others. I was 43 when I came to this realisation and I've never looked back since.

EXERCISE: IKIGAI

Take some time out to ask yourself these four questions.

What do I love doing?

_____

_____

_____

_____

What am I good at?

_____

_____

_____

_____

What does the world need?

_____

_____

_____

_____

What can I get paid for?

_____

_____

_____

_____

Give yourself half an hour to complete this task and contemplate your responses. How do they relate to how you spend your time currently?

Without a self-defined purpose we are lost, unfulfilled and hollow. To understand your purpose, you have to level with yourself: where are you right now and where do you want to be? Until you understand who you are as a person, you won't understand what you really want out of life.

I did well at school up until a certain point when I asked myself, 'What is the fucking point of all this?' Because I couldn't relate to how academia benefited me and what positive end it would lead to, it held no purpose for me. No meaning. I needed a direction and purpose through which I could channel my energy and drive. Fortunately, I found an outlet for it in sport, particularly cross-country running. As a kid, you've got so much energy and drive that needs to attach itself to something positive; unguided it will end up getting you into trouble, which is precisely what happened to me.

I couldn't keep out of it as a teenager, be it petty shoplifting, or stealing a shotgun and wandering around with it under my parka like Burton-on-Trent's answer to Wyatt Earp. My mum managed to get me back into sport and that gave me a much-needed direction, a focus. I was a decent 1,500-metre runner and good at cross-country and she, bless her, would drive me all over the place so I could compete. And once she did that, that took me out of my familiar surroundings and away from the people who said I'd never change, that I was a repeat offender bound for nowhere but jail. My success as a runner gave me positive validation from others, a newfound respect for myself, and a sense of fulfilment. It also made me realise that I could change for the better and didn't have to conform to what others said I would be. Just hearing their predictions made me want to prove them wrong.

Most prisoners in UK jails and, I'd hazard a guess, in most prisons across the world, are youths aged between 18 and 27 years old. The brain is still building itself till around the age of 27, and while the frontal cortex (the part of the brain that does the rationalising and rulemaking) is 'closed for construction till further notice', youths have to rely on their lizard brain. They act out of fear, fight-or-flight behaviour and don't think of the consequences. But another reason they end up in jail is they have no purpose. Consider how many great boxers throughout the sport's history have said they would have ended up in prison had it not been for the discipline of boxing taking them to the gym instead. This was my problem; I just didn't know what the hell to do with all that restlessness and energy. Had it not been for running and my obsession with joining the Royal Marines, I probably wouldn't be here now.

As I said earlier in the book, I didn't find my real purpose until I worked for the Grey Man, helping liberate children from the sex trade. And although it ended abruptly, the silver lining to that cloud was that I had finally discovered that my passion in life was helping others. Victor Frankl was bang on the money!

Think of your goals over the next 12 months, and ask yourself: 'What do I need to add or subtract to help me achieve my goal and lead a happier life?'

THE PURPOSE PYRAMID

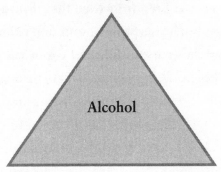

Does it add growth?

Alcohol

Do I enjoy it?   **Does it help others?**

The Purpose Pyramid is a useful tool to measure the worth of anything in your life that may be of questionable merit. This can be something that's a current habit or something that you're negotiating bringing into your life. The central subject matter represents that which you're questioning. As an example I've placed 'alcohol' there, but it might well be 'job', 'relationship', 'business venture' ... in fact, place anything you're not sure about in the centre. Starting at the top ask yourself: 'Does it add personal internal growth to me?' I'm not talking money, but rather does it make you a better human being. When it comes to alcohol and me, I can categorically state that it doesn't make me better – in fact, it makes me worse.

Next: 'Do I enjoy it?' In my case, for example, do I enjoy the three days' muddiness and depression that follows falling off the wagon? No, I don't.

And the last question: 'Does it help others?' Only the landlord of the pub and the managers of the off-licence that I (used to) buy my alcohol from. Certainly, it doesn't benefit me or my loved ones, as I end up being the worst version of myself, grumpy and self-loathing, which is not a good place to operate from.

The subject matter must generate two ticks out of three (minimum) for you to keep it in your life. If it only ticks one or none, you need to bin it sharpish. Always keep this simple triangle in your mind and apply it constantly if you want to be in control of your quality filter.

EXERCISE: THE PURPOSE PYRAMID

Complete your own purpose pyramid. Place an element from your life that is of questionable merit in the middle. Then ask yourself the three questions: Does it add growth? Do I enjoy it? Does it help others? Be honest with yourself.

Does it add growth?

Your concern

Do I enjoy it?   Does it help others?

Does it add growth?

_____

_____

_____

Yes/no: _____

Do I enjoy it?

_____

_____

_____

Yes/no: _____

Does it help others?

_____

_____

_____

Yes/no: _____

Now you've done the exercise, how many yeses did you get?
How many nos? Remember – to keep the thing you're wondering
about in your life, you must answer yes to at least two of these
questions. If you tick only one you must seriously question if it
has a place in your life, or none means that you should bin it
from your life immediately.

EXERCISE: TAKING STOCK OF YOUR LIFE

Question the purpose of each of the topics below, and be as honest as you can:

People in your life: Take a good, hard look at the people you talk to on a regular basis and consider how much quality there is in these friendships and working relationships. I talk to far fewer people now than I did ten years ago. But I tend to talk to people that I care about and who care about me. Some people who I've known for years, I no longer talk to because I realise the effects they have on me are not positive. Although I haven't removed them from my life, they're not part of my daily nutrition.

_____

_____

_____

_____

_____

_____

_____

_____

_____

_____

Your job: If you weigh up the positives against the negatives, how does your chosen employment stack up? What is its purpose, and do you feel aligned to that? Do you feel like you're moving and progressing? Do you feel satisfied? What are your working relationships like? How does your boss treat you? Do you feel inspired or unmotivated? Are you earning what you want to earn? Did you picture yourself doing something else?

_____

_____

_____

_____

_____

_____

_____

_____

_____

By asking these basic questions, 'What's the purpose of this?' or 'Is it having a good or bad effect on me?' we are able to identify the elements in our life that cause us pain or waste our time. Once we identify the negatives that detract from the good in our lives, it makes them much easier to let go of.

When you complete this exercise with any current habit or activity, and also anything you're negotiating in the future, you'll start to get an idea of what's good for you and if you're investing your time in activities that mean something to you, where you get a good deal from your ROI (return on investment) or not.

A person with a self-defined purpose is a force to be reckoned with. Look how I trod water in Brisbane for two years with the oil company. As soon as I had my epiphany about starting a company, within two weeks I had sold up and gone back to a country I swore I'd never visit again. If your *why* is strong enough, you'll flex to any *what* in order to achieve it. Purpose is the engine that drives us. As Bruce Lee, the famous martial artist and movie star, once said: 'A purpose is the eternal condition of success.'

He believed that when we are full of purpose, the pursuit of our goal doesn't feel like hard work but rather the pursuit of becoming ourselves. 'Your main purpose is to become your true self. You don't have to have your purpose figured out but put yourself on a path to find it. Do you feel like you're in the flow or stagnant?' When our purpose is to be true to ourselves, when we are on the right path, our goal becomes easier to achieve.

PART II

BARRIERS TO CHANGE

CHAPTER 4

THE NEGATIVITY DEFAULT

You can't replace a spark plug in a car's engine without knowing what it does and where to find it. Similarly, in order to make successful change within our lives it's vital to know how and why we are hardwired toward certain behaviours and how to challenge them.

LPS (LIFE POSITIONING SYSTEM)

Recently, I was running short on time to get to an appointment – a common occurrence these days. So I jumped into my car, punched in the address on my satnav and headed off sharpish. It took me longer than expected to get there, and by the time I arrived I was extremely late for my appointment. And angry: after the meeting I checked the route and realised the GPS had taken me on a much longer journey than I would have usually taken. I was irked by it, but then I reflected on how stupid *I'd* been, allowing myself to be dictated to by a system that had no real understanding of my needs; it was prepared to take me on a route that avoided the efficiency of the alternative and less-trodden path. I jumped in my car, automatically drifted to autopilot, and let the system tell me where to go without a thought for my own appreciation of the route and time to get there. Does this sound familiar? Is this how your life has become?

That's the curse of modern technology: what it giveth, it taketh away. People are like old horses on a riding-school hack who plod along with their eyes shut, automatically following their old routes. I call this the Life Positioning System. Like GPS, the Life Positioning System points us to where we've already been rather than offering us the road less travelled, which has so much more to teach us. In a rare moment of consciousness when you do pop your head up, you often realise there was a much better route you could have taken, one that was fresh, different and therefore more stimulating and rewarding (and, consequently, more efficient too).

Our default blueprint is to be sheep, to follow the herd, to be lazy and never challenge the status quo. It's easier to mimic other people and fit in and be meek, but with that comes boredom and stagnation. Our reliance on tech is absolute and we now lack the resourcefulness of our forefathers a hundred years ago who had to look at a map to find their destination or use a pencil and paper to do maths. And this is the same with our lives. Sometimes we need to take out a pencil and paper and plan our route.

Most people nonchalantly follow their LPS till the day they die and then wonder on their deathbeds why they're consumed with regret. But how are we to dust off our Life Positioning Systems? Imagine that you were going to die tomorrow night and that life's final gift was to allow you one more day to do, go or be anything you wanted until midnight tomorrow. What would it be?

The best way to wake up and stop falling into your LPS is to meditate regularly (see Chapter 11 for instructions on how to meditate), which allows you to be more aware of yourself, to let yourself be curious, and not take everything for granted, and to be present in the *now*. Question the status quo and look for the direction that feels natural to you and not dictated by others.

The more we understand that as humans we are programmed to be resistant to change – because change represents a threat to our survival – the more obvious are the many barriers we erect to stop it happening; even when it is a necessary change that will make us happier. To become Battle Ready, we need to be versatile and flexible to deal with what is thrown at us and to seize opportunities, and that means embracing change. We'll come back to my own story and the bootcamp I designed in order to achieve my goal and follow my purpose on my return to England, but over the next few chapters we're going to learn about how the brain works and the mechanisms within us that operate automatically. In this chapter let's take a closer look at the barriers we need to navigate in order to break out of our not-so-comfortable comfort zones.

THE SURVIVAL BLUEPRINT

As humans, our primary focus is survival, and to this end we've evolved to live in a state of near-constant fear and vigilance; we're as wired to negativity as wasps drawn to an open bottle of Coke, always looking for something that will go wrong, forever anxious with *what ifs?* Blame it on our distant ancestors, but fear and self-doubt have kept us alive ever since we left the safety of the trees to make our imprint on the world 2.5 million years ago. Back then, we weren't top of the food chain and we couldn't afford to be over complacent – there were cave bears and sabre-tooth tigers looking to feed on us each time we left our cave.

Then 1.8 million years ago we caught a break and discovered fire, which in turn enabled us to cook and sophisticate the diversity of our diets thereby developing the human brain. Fire also helped keep predators at bay and allowed us humans to stay up later and develop communication and intellectual thought.

Fast-forward to around 300,000 years BC and early mankind was able to use wood and stone tools effectively, build shelters and had also begun to talk to each other with basic grunts (sounds like the Marines!). Anatomically modern humans emerged about 200,000 years ago, but it wasn't until around 50,000 years ago that our species enjoyed an explosion of innovation, with much improved weaponry, and the advancement of language developed to such an extent that we could communicate very precisely what we wanted, which resulted in culture becoming more complex and structured.

Despite all these developments mankind is still hardwired to fear. In our 2.8 million-year journey to where we are now, 99.9 per cent of that time has been spent evolving under dangerous circumstances – as little as 15,000 years ago we were *still* being hunted by predators! It's no wonder certain modes of behaviour, like the 'fight-or-flight' syndrome still dominate our reactions even in situations where we're no longer in mortal danger. Look at what happens in a moment of road rage – one moment a person is listening to Smooth FM, then someone cuts him up and he regresses to behaving like a caveman. Chemicals within the body create the symptoms of fight or flight – shaky hands, weak leg muscles, increased heartbeat, churning stomach, loss of breath and sweating palms – through increased cortisol (stress hormone) and testosterone (fight hormone), which hijack the blood flow, oxygen and synaptic activity in your brain responsible for making you act rationally; putting it instead into the limbic system which is home to the instinctive amygdala part of your brain, where fear is processed and anger is triggered. One driver goes into *fight* mode and 'sees red', while the other *flies* for their life and hurriedly drives off.

Fear dominates our lives on a daily basis: fear of failure, fear of what others think, fear of missing out, fear of getting older, fear of success, fear of the dark ... the possibilities are almost endless, amplified by the constant drone of negativity staged by the media on your TV, newspaper and social media. Given then that we're now top of the food chain, and tragically most of the animals with teeth who can eat us are on the verge of extinction, why are we still enchained to fear?

Consider the speed with which we have evolved over the last 2,500 years; relative to our slowly morphing ancestors, the apes, it's safe to say that time and technology have overtaken our general evolution. Which is dangerous. 'Tech' has become so much an integral part of our lives and is developing so rapidly that we can no longer control it or live without it. When the geeks in Silicon Valley quietly admit that they won't let their kids near the stuff they design because it's too addictive, and Elon Musk, the man taking us to Mars in 2030, believes creating artificial intelligence is akin to summoning the devil, you know we're in over our heads!

The human survival blueprint, like that of many animal species, is still hardwired to fear as a means of survival, which results in us avoiding taking fresh new paths when a familiar well-trodden one can be followed instead. It also means we're not fulfilling our potential and leading the full lives we might. Taking the untrodden path towards new experiences is our birth right. Humans are brilliant creatures and creators – we've built sky-defying monuments to our gods, cured diseases, established free healthcare, mapped and even visited the heavens, but we are still pale, half creatures unnecessarily cowering by the firelight in the cave, and falling well short of our true potential, outside in the brilliant sunshine. Once we learn to understand our genetic make-up and how as humans we've been designed to think and feel, we can more easily recognise when our default fear mechanism is depriving us of a new experience.

THE SHORTCUT SYNDROME

The Shortcut Syndrome is something we're all guilty of and can all relate to. As humans, we tend to want the end result without doing the work necessary to achieve it. We're wired to take the easy path and avoid stress at all costs. Take surfing, for instance. Learning how to surf is a time-sapping and humiliating process. I have several boards and even own a surf van, but can I surf? No! Surfing, like almost everything worthwhile, is one thing that you can't shortcut, it takes time and effort to gain any knowledge and skill of the art. It's about persistence. My failure is linked to my inability to see purpose in the outcome of surfing. Yes, I'm sure it would be cool and very satisfying, but until you get the taste of success you fail to see the need and purpose, and purpose alone is the one thing that drives anyone to achieve their goals. One day I'll be able to surf, as soon as it ascends to the top of my goal-setting priorities.

Colin Wilson, a great twentieth-century thinker, believed we live our lives in a sleepwalk, only waking in rare moments when we are stimulated by something that allows us off the treadmill. He said:

> Human beings are 99 per cent 'robot'. Our bodies are programmed to breathe, to sleep, digest, excrete; our instincts are programmed to reproduce our kind and protect our children. But our minds are also mechanical ... I am typing this page without effort, because after thirty-odd years, typing has become 'automatic'. We live automatically. The simplest way of ceasing to live 'mechanically' is to make a continual attempt at 'vigilance', self-awareness.

The drive to satisfy our primal obligations of food, sleep and procreation take priority over everything else, and in order to ensure these fundamentals are met, the mind takes shortcuts. As soon as you walk into a new situation it will make a few rapid enquiries in your memory bank to try to connect the present situation to something similar you have experienced before; an approximation, a shortcut. And if it can't find an appropriate example, to ensure you're still fit to fulfil your primal obligations it will send you fear to avoid your attempts at trying something new. We often experience a sense of fear disproportionate to the situation.

What we perceive as the real world around us, we're in fact viewing through a lens of our past experiences that are attached with corresponding emotions. This is a subjective way of seeing new experiences, where we filter anything new through all our past hurts and joys, successes and failures, so our response to the new thing is tinged by what we have been through in the past. We need to make a conscious attempt to view new things objectively, to perceive them happening as they are around us, rather than being 'automatic' in our response.

While the left side of our brain deals in logic, is more aware of time strictures and prone to worry, the right side – if we'd only allow it, through slowing our breath and relaxing – comes to our aid delivering clarity and calm. In pressured situations, our panic mechanism kicks in as we ask ourselves, *How do I get out of this?* We need to recognise the behaviour and breathe our way out of it, until the fear has subsided. As I mentioned in the first chapter, while I was in the Special Forces I learned a trick I named 'Breathe, Recalibrate and Deliver'. In moments of stress or when you have a mental blockage you want to navigate around, just by breathing slowly and consciously you can slow yourself down to a state of calm, and from this position you're able to make a rational, focused decision.

When I have to get up and start my daily routine at 5 a.m., my body says no. So I breathe, recalibrate and take action within a few seconds, otherwise my brain will support the opposite. Focus on why you need to get up, get fit, meditate. Don't dally, don't' think for long, just GET UP! Breathe – recalibrate – deliver.

THE EGO

'The ego is a veil between what you think you are and what you actually are. You live under the illusion of the mind, totally unaware that you are directed by a great big load of stories!'

– Isira Sananda

In the Special Forces, it is assumed that operators have little or no ego, but that would be a false statement. What they do possess is the ability to be aware of the ego, to know when it is unbalanced in a situation and be able to control its output. I've met some of the most humble but dangerous men while in the Special Forces, all capable of inflicting severe pain and destruction, but who have the ability to back down to a weaker opponent when the greater good was at stake.

The ego is your self-image of who you *think* you are, a construct of the mind based on your beliefs, talents and experiences. The ego separates you as being distinctly different than the things around you, leaving you disconnected. We take heed of the ego's incessant voice in our mind, believing everything it tells us, even though it is driven by the need to be liked and to feel good about itself and will happily bullshit you to satisfy that end. It lives in the past, reliving old triumphs, and in the future where it pictures owning yet more glittery things – a better car, a boat, a bigger house – but it's never enough, for once you've attained what it lusts after, the ego gets bored, feels unsatisfied and those glittery things become empty and worthless. The present is never good enough for the ego, it's continually projecting forward, thinking it will be happy when it has attained this or that. The more we submit to the mindless religion of consumerism, the more debt we get ourselves into and the more enchained we are to the wheel of predictability. We're addicted to owning stuff that supports the perception of who we want to be. It's as if it is in our DNA.

Imagine you were the last person on Earth. Would your choice of car, clothes and material objects change, given there was no one to impress? Would it become practical rather than flash?

The ego is a diva driven by an insecure need for constant recognition from others. Eckhart Tolle, one of the most well-known spiritual teachers on the planet, suggests the ego's identification with *things* begins as toddlers when we become territorial over a toy, 'That's mine!' This need to identify with possessions deepens in adulthood, the need to be defined by what we possess becomes almost an obsession. On a greater scale of ego, consider the behaviour of countries and their need to possess other countries in order to feel strong. In his book, *A New Earth*, Tolle says:

> *Fear, greed and the desire for power are the psychological motivating forces not only behind warfare and violence between nations, tribes, religions and ideologies, but also the cause of conflict in personal relationships. They bring about an illusion in your perception of other people and yourself.*

You could argue that Western society has become lost because it has engorged itself with material possessions, and an overfocus on money. Bhutan, in stark contrast, is a little-known principality deep in the Himalayas, sandwiched between Tibet and India. In 1971, its forward-thinking king rejected GDP (Gross Domestic Product) in favour of GNH (Gross National Happiness), which seeks to measure prosperity by the spiritual, physical, social and environmental well-being of its citizens. The idea that inner health and the preservation of the environment take precedence over material growth is unique. While the remainder of the world has screwed itself with corporate greed, overdevelopment and a lack of care for the earth we live in, Bhutan is like a different planet.

In business, I have chosen to focus, where possible, on what my company does and why, not just what it earns. And while I project what its earnings will be next year, I also consider the people the business is going to positively affect, be it veterans or civilians. Helping others is my passion, and I believe if I hold true to my passion, the profits necessary to keep the company successful will follow. If, like Bhutan, we were to ask ourselves: *How am I going to create happiness?* as opposed to, *How am I going to create wealth?* we would be more fulfilled.

In his book, *Stillness Speaks*, Tolle suggests that once we learn to recognise our ego's inner voice and observe our thinking mind, we will start to wake up and free ourselves from the ego. This newfound awareness connects us to the present, the essence of who we really are. A Zen monk might describe this as going beyond thinking. Picture a conversation with someone. How present are you as you listen to them? Are you interested in them and curious to hear what happens next, or are you waiting for your cue to speak about yourself? Are you judging and imposing your mental labels on them?

Our modern conception of the ego is derived from the Latin *ego*, meaning 'I', and true to form the ego is purely self-oriented. Sometimes I catch myself feeling jealous when a friend has had some good news. Then I step out of myself and observe what's going on: it's my ego at work, threatened by another's success. I remind myself that my focus and achievement is my training company, and then that horrible green-eyed snake in my guts slithers away. Social networks like Instagram, Twitter and Facebook are platforms of instant validation and gratification and are fertile fields for the ego because we measure our success as people by how many likes we've received for a comment or photo we posted.

After we pass our physical prime in our twenties, the brightness of our looks begins to fade. From an evolutionary standpoint, we no longer need to procreate, we're supposed to have done that by the time we're 30, so nature doesn't require us to be so physically attractive. We grow wrinkled and grey on the outside but hopefully wiser on the inside. And yet the world is so obsessed with looks, and vanity so integrally linked to self-worth, that many men and women refuse to grow old gracefully, taking Botox fillers and hair transplants in an attempt to cheat time and be like Peter Pan. Again, the ego fears its relevance will be diluted if it no longer gets the attention it has always enjoyed. Self-worth can become defined by how others perceive us. The sooner we realise the fakery and false reality of the ego, and learn to listen out for its voice, the sooner we will see that the things it tells us are not reality at all. That true self-worth lies in the happiness of the inner self.

How many times have you argued with a loved one and over-reacted in such a way that when the dust settled and the threat has diminished, the feelings of guilt and regret play heavily on your mind? You've just had a visit from your ego in its self-defensive survival mode; always ready to attack, defend and retaliate. Until I became aware of my ego, I thought I was showing early signs of madness because of this relentless ongoing conflict in my mind.

When I understood how crippling it could be, I made a conscious effort to always be aware of what was going on in my thought process and emotions. I used the Breathe, Recalibrate and Deliver skill I learned in the Special Forces to help regain control. Just by rationalising and questioning my reaction for a few seconds I could determine if it was my ego at the driving seat or myself. The ability to pause for a second in the heat of battle is the key to dominating any enemy.

Sadly, our ego doesn't go away, it's an inherent part of what makes us human, but we do have a choice whether to engage with it or not. The more familiar you get with the symptoms of its arrival the closer you'll become to your inner consciousness, your real self. Here's a useful little checklist to identify when your ego has taken over.

10 SIGNS THAT YOUR EGO IS IN THE DRIVING SEAT

- You feel empowered by gossiping about other people's flaws.
- A heated discussion turns into an argument because you can't back down until you've won.
- You constantly judge others, when another is poorer, smaller, less fortunate than you.
- You feel threatened when someone is better at something, has more money than you, is more popular, better-looking, wealthier.
- You feel jealous when others do well, find it hard to congratulate them and feel threatened.
- You feel the need to talk about yourself when someone has been talking about themselves and their success.
- If you can't win, you prefer not to be involved.

- When you don't win a challenge you sulk, rather than be content that you've done your best.
- You set yourself impossible goals and beat yourself up when you don't reach them.
- You blame failures on other people, it's always someone else's fault, and you are always right.

When you see people who have done remarkably well in life, you rarely find them acting out any of the above behaviours. They don't need to brag, in fact they're often loath to talk about themselves. They are curious about other people, humble and open to learning new things without feeling self-conscious. They're also generous listeners and listen to understand rather than to be heard. People who keep their egos in check seem more at home with themselves, comfortable in their skin and happy to be in the moment. The ego must be balanced with judgement and mindfulness otherwise your thoughts will create feelings, which in turn create actions that are counterproductive. The ego's a relationship killer, dream wrecker and is to blame for the downfall of many a great individual who lost their way because they started believing the hype in themselves and allowed their ego to bloat.

EXERCISE: EGO THE DIVA

Your first step toward inner consciousness is to start recognising that the ego is not you, and there is a quieter stillness within you that comes to the fore in moments when you become an observer of the ego or quieten its chatter through meditation. Start keeping a mental record of when the ego takes over. Think about what triggered this behaviour and how you could have acted in a nobler way. Most importantly be conscious. When you learn to recognise the ego you can stop it in its tracks and decide whether it is needed in the current situation or not at all. It's the same for all emotions, which can at times be highly inflammatory.

Note down three occasions when your ego has flared up and taken over your rational self.

1. _____

_____

_____

2. _____

_____

_____

3. _____

_____

_____

Now think about each occasion according to the following questions:

What were the signs?

1. _____

_____

_____

2. _____

_____

_____

3. _____

_____

_____

How did you feel?

1. _____

_____

_____

2. _____

_____

_____

3. _____

_____

_____

Were you in control?

1. _____

_____

_____

2. _____

_____

_____

3. _____

_____

_____

What was the effect it had on the other person(s)?

1. _____

_____

_____

2. _____

_____

_____

3. _____

_____

_____

How did you feel afterwards when your ego had climbed back in its crib?

1. _____

_____

_____

2. _____

_____

_____

3. _____

_____

_____

Now, replay those three scenarios but this time without the ego. How would the impact/result be any different?

1. _____

_____

_____

_____

2. _____

_____

_____

_____

3. _____

_____

_____

_____

THE SUBCONSCIOUS

Imagine an iceberg. We see perhaps 5 per cent of it poking above the surface, and the rest, about 95 per cent, is under water. Our brains are like icebergs, with 5 per cent – the bit you can see – representing our conscious mind, but the rest of its power – 95 per cent of it – lies hidden under the surface in the subconscious.

Using another metaphor, think of your subconscious like an underground storage facility (picture the vast warehouse at the end of *Raiders of the Lost Ark*), where all your memories, experiences, fears, hopes, regrets and beliefs are carefully catalogued. The subconscious is not just a reference library, however, there's also a vast garden above that will bloom into anything you want depending on the messages you feed it. The subconscious never sleeps. It works nights configuring dreams to solve puzzles and rehearse events you might be worrying about, and quietly goes about realising the thoughts you've been actively or passively posting to it throughout the day.

The subconscious helps us achieve our goals, and while you might think training it is about as easy as wrangling a mustang in pitch-black darkness, it's more achievable than you think. If you're unconsciously dreading an upcoming exam and picture yourself on the day staring emptily into space, lost for words, this is the message you're inputting into your subconscious, your expectation, and it's what it will act out for you, for the subconscious doesn't know the difference between negatives and positives. But if, on the other hand, your intention is to be prepared, and you lucidly picture yourself answering the exam questions with ease, your subconscious will ensure you put in the requisite revision time and deliver exactly what you pictured.

By feeding the subconscious with the right key messages on a regular basis, visualising the outcomes we desire in a very precise way, we can impress our goals upon it so it actively helps us achieve them. Neglecting the subconscious is akin to leaving a toddler alone with a pair of scissors and a pot of super glue: it will create its own results, however disastrous.

The frontal cortex, where we do our immediate thinking, is the feeder to the subconscious, it's where we do most of our initial planning and can handle around five to nine bits of information at a time, but this breaks down to one or two when in a pressured situation. Once you have an idea and an intention is set, time should be allowed for the subconscious to process and start to focus on achieving the goal.

The ego and the subconscious are vital parts of our psyche, but the trick is to make sure that you're the one who's in the driving seat. As soon as you let the ego take the wheel, you'll soon find yourself subject to a sense of self-worth that's based on what other people think about you, rather than one based on self-belief. And if you give your subconscious the right instructions, it will direct you where you want to go; but if you neglect it, you will soon find yourself somewhere you didn't want to be.

CHAPTER 5

IT'S ALL IN YOUR HEAD

n this chapter we'll look at the old grey matter, how it's composed and how we can reshape it and fool it into action.

I spent a long time thinking about my life and how the machine works. A mechanic first has to understand the way the engine works in order to conduct a diagnosis, compile a fault report and subsequently fix the problem before it gets any worse. We are fixated on how we look and train our physical bodies to give the image of health and happiness. However, the need to do this often stems from what's going on in our brains. Looking good should be a by-product of feeling good and time spent understanding how the brain works will allow self-diagnosis, prevention and cure. The brain is the conduit to your happiness but also your sorrow. Learning to control this part of the machine will help you not only maintain a healthy mental balance but will also allow you to achieve exactly what you desire.

If you want to be Battle Ready, this is where it starts.

UNDERSTANDING THE BRAIN

The human brain is one of the most complex structures in the Universe. Home to 100 billion neurons, it can store more data – up to 1,000 terabytes! – than your average library.

In simple terms, there are three different brains that make up the whole. The **Brain Stem**, also known as the Reptilian Brain, is the oldest, and governs our breathing, heart rate, blood pressure and hunger as well as thirst, pain, smell, sleep, wakefulness and sexual urges. Responsible for our general survival, it is fuelled by fear – fear of failure, being alone, being left behind, being taken advantage of, financial difficulty, or not achieving goals. It shuts down the other two brains and takes control when it perceives we're in danger, using fight-or-flight behaviour to get us out of trouble as quickly as possible.

The second brain is the **Emotional Brain**, also known as the limbic system or Mammalian Brain. Unlike reptiles, which lay their eggs then bugger off to eat, sleep or have sex, mammals look after their newborns, nurture and teach them, just as the mammalian part of our brain is driven by the need to care for others, build community and feel empathy. It wants to be empowered, to know that it is making a positive impact on the world. Love, anger, jealousy, happiness, hate, pride and all other higher emotions are felt here.

The third brain is called the **Cortical Brain**, or neo-cortex, and is responsible for rationality, planning ahead, memory, imagination and reining in our impulses. This is the most recently formed part of the brain and what makes us human. However, it is the oldest part, the Reptilian Brain that is boss, for our instinct for survival is paramount above all other considerations. The next strongest is the Emotional Brain and these first two work well together and form the subconscious. The Cortical Brain comes a poor third. Not surprisingly, the brain has been likened to an animal menagerie, home to a lizard, horse and human all trying to inhabit the same body.

NEUROPLASTICITY

As little as 25 years ago, neurologists believed that except for injuries sustained in accidents, the brain experienced no active changes after puberty. How wrong they were! 'Neuroplasticity' refers to the brain's ability to restructure itself, creating new neural pathways and synapses to adapt to damage to the brain, and to new environments and when learning something new. If the left side of the brain, which controls speech, is damaged, the right side may pick up some of the slack to help. Imagine a narrow country lane that grows into a super-highway and you are getting close to the potential possibilities of creating new neural pathways.

'Neurogenesis' is the process whereby new neurons (brain cells) are grown as a result of quality sleep, regular exercise and sex. Other activities that promote neurogenesis include reading, playing a musical instrument, eating blueberries, and – you'll be glad to hear – eating dark chocolate, as well as stimulating our mind through travel, learning a new language, and challenging our comfort zones. In other words, not just switching off and sleepwalking, but constantly arousing stimulation in our brains through careful consideration of what we put into our mind, body and gut. The human gut, where we experience those powerful instinctual feelings that often guide us, is home to more neurons than you'll find in a cat's brain!

Joe Dispenza in his book *You Are The Placebo: Making Your Mind Matter* asserts that 80 to 90 per cent of our thoughts are the same as those we had yesterday, making us hardwired to the past. In our biology, hormones, neurocircuitry and neurochemistry are informed by how we think, act and feel. Thought leads to action. Our thoughts invade us the moment we wake up, immediately veering to the negative as they focus on problems. Those problems are associated with people and places and attached to each is a corresponding feeling. As soon as we access this memory bank, the data of the past, we're prone to repeat old thoughts, which then produce old feelings of anxiety and fear.

In his book Dispenza says:

Thoughts are the language of the brain and feelings the language of the body; how you think and feel creates your state of being. Your body is your unconscious mind and doesn't know the difference between an experience in your life that creates an emotion, and an emotion that you can create by thought alone.

He goes on to say that if you are reliving the same emotions over and over again, you are limiting your thinking, you will become trapped in the past and you will be unable to see future possibility.

* * *

In 1986, Joe Dispenza was riding his bike in the cycling stage of a triathlon when he was hit by a truck. He broke six vertebrae, which scattered bone fragments across his spinal cord. Doctors informed him he probably wouldn't walk again. Rejecting their offer of a metal frame that would be grafted to his spine, he focused instead on one thought: 'The power that made the body, heals the body.' Then back at home, he set to work connecting with the innate intelligence within him that had created his body and started telling it what to do. For two hours a day he would picture his healed spine, visualising the vertebrae one-by-one, as healthy and strong. Within eleven weeks he was back in the office without any surgery or the aid of a back brace.

WE'RE AS YOUNG AS WE THINK WE ARE!

Journalist Anil Ananthaswamy reports on fascinating research that shows how important your mindset is in influencing the ageing process. In 1979, Ellen Langer, now a Harvard University psychology professor, invited two groups of elderly men to visit a New Hampshire monastery. One group lived inside a time capsule: everything about their week-long retreat was dialled back to reflect 1959. The other group was told to reminisce but given no specific instructions or stimulation from any era.

The control group showed no physical or biological differences. The men told to live like they did 20 years ago, however, 'looked younger in the after-pictures.' That's not all. 'When Langer studied the men after a week of such sensory and mindful immersion in the past, she found that their memory, vision, hearing, and even physical strength had improved,' writes Ananthaswamy.

Langer never published her results. She didn't have the funding to properly control the second group and didn't want to release her data in a second-rate journal, but the experience never left her mind. Years later, she conducted a study on patients with Type 2 diabetes. Forty-six subjects played computer games for an hour and a half. They had to switch games every 15 minutes. One group had a properly working clock; one had a clock that kept time slowly; while the last group had a clock that was sped up. Langer wanted to know if their blood sugar levels would follow real or perceived time. Incredibly, perceived time won out. How each subject thought about time influenced the metabolic processes inside of their bodies.

Ananthaswamy writes that people between the ages of 40 and 80 tend to feel younger than their chronological age, while those in their twenties feel older. This makes sense, as Robert Sapolsky points out in *Behave*: after the age of 30 our metabolism slows down, which skews our perception of time. Time actually *feels* different. What's amazing about the research above is we have a conscious decision in how we feel about that.

Florida State University College of Medicine psychologist and gerontologist Antonio Terracciano states subjective age is correlated with factors such as walking speed, lung capacity, grip strength, and bodily inflammation. As Langer's work, among others, shows, it's not necessarily the body influencing the mind. Your mindset about ageing has an equally important role in aging. Terracciano's research has shown that this affects cognition: a belief in a higher subjective age correlates with cognitive impairments and even dementia, prompting this advice.

If people think that because they are getting older they cannot do things, cut their social ties, or incorporate this negative view which limits their life, that can be really detrimental. While fighting those negative attitudes, challenging yourself, keeping an open mind, being engaged socially, can absolutely have a positive impact. So much can be revealed by how we talk about ourselves. How much emphasis do you place on numerical age? Do you believe age limits your physical and mental abilities? Is age an excuse for all the new things you don't try? Do you spend more time reminiscing about what once was instead of planning on what's to come? These questions are indicative of the mindset you have around age. And, as this research shows, will affect how you actually age.

A friend of mine was an author for Lonely Planet guidebooks when he developed Parkinson's disease at the age of 40. He was fit, an ex-amateur boxer, and one of the publisher's go-to writers for taking on rugged and sometimes dangerous countries that demanded a level of physical grit. With a young family to support, he tried to keep going at his usual pace, taking assignments one after the next, a schedule that would have been punishing for someone who wasn't balancing an illness. His body began to slow down, he was running on empty. In despair, he had himself admitted to a double-blind placebo drug trial to assess the efficacy of an existing diabetes drug that was based on the saliva of a Gila monster; a Mexican lizard that eats only three times a year. Half of the participants in this trial would be taking the real drug, while the remainder would unknowingly be injecting themselves with nothing but water.

That year he took on an absurd amount of travel work, much of it in jungles and mountains that required a higher than usual level of fitness. Believing himself to be benefiting from the drug, he felt more like his old self and experienced an enhanced level of well-being and energy as he worked in the jungles of Borneo and Laos. Come the end of the trial the results were positive: the speed and precision of his motor skills had improved by 19 per cent. He was convinced his recovery was down to the 'lizard spit', however it turned out he'd been on the placebo all the time. The challenge was to keep up the progress he'd made in his body now that he knew it was down to him and no outside agency; for 18 months he'd fed his brain with the message that it was getting better thanks to the Exenatide drug, but now that he knew that wasn't the case he neglected to instruct it to keep healing itself and quickly lapsed back into the clutches of the disease, whereupon his symptoms got worse again.

In 1969, Bruce Lee severely injured his back during a routine training session because he had not warmed-up sufficiently. He was told he might never walk normally again and could forget about practising martial arts. After a period of depression, restricted to his bed and able to do nothing, Lee resolved to reject the prognosis of the doctors and get to know his body better in order to try and heal it. He read up on nutrition, kinesiology, biomechanics and yoga, anything that might strengthen his goal of walking again. As a constant affirmation to combat self-doubt during his recovery, he wrote several specific goals on the back of business cards and placed them on his bedroom wall. One read: 'walk on', another that he would become the first Asian American action movie star.

Given his condition, it might have seemed like a preposterously lofty ambition. Yet within a year of self-prescribed exercises, positive thinking and constant visualisation, Bruce Lee was healed. Of his self-imposed recovery, he wrote: 'But with every adversity comes a blessing, because a shock acts as a reminder to oneself that we must not get stale in routine.' Lee also went on to star in *Enter the Dragon*, the first big-budget American Chinese Kung Fu film, which instantly made him the most famous Pan-Asian movie star in the world (tragically, he died a month before its release).

We *can* heal ourselves through clear intention, and careful management of the thoughts we seed our subconscious with. If you can visualise the way you want to feel by imagining it clearly, you'll begin to feel as if it has already happened. And just by feeling like this your reality will start to change for the better.

New conscious thoughts lead to new behaviours, begetting fresh experiences and new emotions. The problem is that traumas we may have experienced, like my chimp attack, make the strongest impressions on our long-term memories, forcing our brain to focus on them again and again, as if they are tattooed on to our Reptile Brain, our fear place. With every memory – good or bad – comes an accompanying feeling, which is why so many people live in continual pain, reliving old feelings that lock them into depression and cause addiction as a means of escape. The first step to flipping unhelpful, outdated thoughts and emotions, is to become an observer of ourselves and our thinking. Dispenza warns that most of us will cling to the familiar rather than embrace the unknown, however unpleasant the familiar might make us feel, holding onto those old thought patterns and emotions of guilt, self-loathing, whatever it might be.

Remember that poor bugger Sisyphus in the Greek underworld, who as punishment had to push a boulder up a hill only to have it roll down, whereupon he had to start again. He was locked in the same action for eternity. In the same vein, if we don't challenge ourselves with new experiences, fresh choices, and meaningful goals, nothing will change and everything in our body and brain will stay the same. Most of us live in near-constant 'survival mode' because we are fuelled by unconscious fear and are hardwired to expect the negative, which in turn triggers stress hormones and the fight-or-flight mechanism in the reptile part of the brain. In this state the brain becomes incoherent and out of rhythm with itself and the body.

COMFORT ZONES

We should embrace short-term discomfort for long-term gain. However we're hardwired to take short-term comfort and this leads to long-term pain.

Being Battle Ready is about dealing with things as and when they present themselves. This usually means dealing with a level of short-term discomfort, otherwise we tend to allow ourselves to become comfortable with the discomfort of yet another thing we haven't attended to. An unpaid bill, an important email not replied to, the untidiness of our home or workspace. When these things get left we adapt to accept them and allow them to be the construct that is our lives. If your life is a list of 'do it laters' and mostly a disorganised mess, when something big happens it will knock you so far off track you won't be able to sustain progression on a chosen path.

We live in comfort zones because they're safe, but that doesn't mean they're good for us (remember that Brisbane mansion with Sarah, and her poisonous ways?). As soon as we're faced with the unknown, be it the chance of a new career, moving abroad, meeting new people, or leaving a relationship that has gone sour, our Mind, ever-guiding us toward safety, sends us the sensation of fear, apprehension and self-doubt to keep us stuck where we are. *Imagine if this goes wrong ... Better the devil you know ...* The Mind wants us to do exactly what we did yesterday and the day before; as far as it's concerned, whatever we've been doing has kept us alive. The problem is that the Mind doesn't give a monkey's whether you're happy or sad – you're alive, and that's all that matters. Job done.

But it's not done, is it? Because in your current 'perceived' comfort zone, you may feel half-dead, bored shitless or terribly unhappy; maybe you're being bullied, drowning in the pub to muffle the existential nausea, or losing yourself in pornography to help paper over the void? Maybe you live in a golden cage and are married to someone who abuses you. A comfort zone might seem like a safe option, but really it's nothing more than a Venus flytrap that keeps you stuck in the same place, all the while sucking the life out of you. Shit smells but it's warm.

Comfort zones are not comfortable at all, but stagnant places where you tread water. Maybe we should refer to them instead as familiar zones, for that's all they are. A crack addict living in a squat strewn with faeces and used hypodermics is in a familiar zone, and his mind may even tell him he's done well to find a spot out of the rain, rent-free, where he can not only use in peace but his dealer also comes to him. Result! The fact that he's still alive is all he cares about, even if the quality of that life barely qualifies as an existence.

The cliché tells us it's 'better the devil you know', but that's bullshit. The key to a satisfying life is pushing ourselves out of that stagnant place into somewhere fresh and new. As we'll see in the next chapter, you can generate whatever you desire in your life, but only if you're prepared to come out of your comfort zone

Fear of change holds back the richness of our experiences. It's peculiar, but most of us in our society play it safe while at the same time we celebrate free spirits, polar explorers, actors and Special Forces soldiers, all of whom take risks. Why do so many of us return to the same place for our holiday, year upon year? Because it's predictable and we know exactly what to expect. But as we've seen, it is only when the brain comes across something novel that it becomes stimulated and produces fresh neurons and thought responses. No wonder travelling somewhere new and exotic is so memorable, for once we've got over the culture shock of spicy smells, people speaking a language we don't understand, and survived, the brain allows itself to be inspired and we start absorbing everything around us with a fresh pair of eyes and a sense of excitement.

People from the corporate sector who come on my training courses are placing themselves in an area of discomfort. They're in unfamiliar and unpredictable surroundings, so their egos are forced to disappear. In these moments their thoughts, feelings and emotions become organic. This is a true reflection of raw character. They don't get the opportunity to design the perfect outcome that will make them look good and avoids any chance of them looking weak or inferior. For most this is a hard pill to swallow; however it is a life-changing one. Parallel with this they are tasked to work with others towards a common goal, some of whom they don't get on with back in the regular office environment. All the comfort-zone behaviour and ill-feeling of the workplace gets flushed away as people start thinking as a team due to an element of vulnerability and expressing themselves more truthfully. In this climate people start to bond. That's why the military is so close because it's void of ego; it's about getting through the situation without any of these external comfort zone factors being relied upon.

EXERCISE: COMFORT ZONE

Make a list of comfort zones you consider yourself to inhabit.

_____

_____

_____

_____

_____

_____

Now write five things about each one which are not positive. Ask yourself what you would need to do to turn these negatives into positives. Would you need to leave the comfort zone to achieve this?

Comfort zone: _____

1. _____

2. _____

3. _____

4. _____

5. _____

How can you turn these negatives into positives?

_____

_____

_____

_____

_____

_____

Would you need to leave your comfort zone?

_____

_____

_____

_____

_____

_____

BREAK POINT: SHORT-TERM DISCOMFORT FOR LONG-TERM GAIN

A 'break point' is an intentional stopping-point in a computer program, designed to debug and get rid of surplus data before carrying on. In the Special Forces, a break point is used to Breathe, Recalibrate and Deliver in a pressured situation in order to engage the courage required to accomplish the uncomfortable. It's the difference between blind panic and taking control of your environment before it spirals out of control; a window of opportunity before the negative default takes over and turns away from a positive breakthrough.

Officer cadets at Sandhurst Training Academy are taught to 'Take a Knee' when approaching obstacles. The term comes from literally getting closer to the ground so the bullets whizzing over your head don't hit you, and consciously putting yourself in a peaceful place where for a moment you can think calmly in order to choose the best option going forward. We always have options available to us, but most of the time we're working under such pressure that we don't slow down sufficiently to realise there is always a crossroads rather than the narrow path we're fixed to.

A break point is when you decide to step out of your comfort zone and grow as a person, accepting that where you're going involves adapting to new territory. You know that your mind will tell you you're going to fail and that it's unsafe, but you'll do it anyway. It's about tolerating the short-term discomfort of change for long-term gain.

Break points happen to us every day in less dramatic circumstances: do we pay that bill that's been bothering us and take charge of our lives, or take the usual shortcuts? Do we talk to the person we've fallen out with at work, or let the disconnect fester into long-term mutual dislike? Do we make a conscious change and go the extra mile, or follow the same old path? I latched on to the term 'break point' when I was living in Australia. At the time I'd started to realise that for years of using drink and drugs and chasing adrenalin highs in war zones in order to feel alive, I'd been a fugitive on the run from the real me. *Who am I?* I wondered.

My recovery began with the self-admission that I had a problem I needed to address. It wasn't the world that was broken and needed fixing, it was me. I began to look inwards instead of listening to my egotistical mind chatter, which was overflowing in anger, self-loathing, fear and desperation. I'd drunk myself into a cul-de-sac of blackouts from three-day binges that barely masked the pain, only for it to return with bigger teeth. But as soon as I started looking inwards for the answers all these positive molecules seemed to grow and coalesce, creative ideas started flowing, and out of nowhere the idea of a company called Break-Point came to me.

We all have moments of clarity where break points appear, the mist thins and we're presented with a route of escape from the situation we're stuck in. The trick is to realise that we have the power within us to follow these routes. I was caught in the web of a bad relationship, too scared to leave it because of the pain and toxic arguments that would follow: instead of experiencing that short-term discomfort for long-term gain, I was prepared to tolerate the flatline of long-term discomfort. We're all tuned that way, with our work, jobs, friendships and marriages ... we must understand the concept of a break point, to push through those moments of discomfort and then see a better future. An extreme example of this is my being attacked by the chimp; I could have accepted my fate and let the ape kill me or fought back and found a break point.

Break Point is about changing the way we think as people. It's the moment you decide nothing will stand between you and your goals and you're prepared to step into the discomfort in the short term for the long-term gain. Like going to the dentist: some will tolerate long-term toothache in preference of the short-term pain of having the tooth extracted, which will end their suffering. In this space, you'll never be creative, nor develop past the person you are currently because you're caught in the fear of the survival blueprint. Until I changed my thinking, I had financial pressure, emotional pressure, relationship pressure ... all these pressures, and I just couldn't get anywhere in life.

A break point allows you to look at yourself and question your situation, helping you realise that there's more to life than maintaining this degree of unhappiness and that you can break free. Think how many people stay in bad relationships to preserve the happiness of their kids, when actually the kids would rather their parents were happy and single than two miserable people staying together for the wrong reason. We're only here once. How old do we have to get before we realise that life is not supposed to be a punishment, and that we have the keys to open the cage we've unwittingly made for ourselves?

I was committed to making my new business work because I was sick of working for other people and having no sense of meaningful purpose. When I was working as a project manager in Brisbane, I was so busy earning a living I didn't have time to take charge of my own destiny. I was just existing. I believe life drives us where we need to be, and it sends to us whatever we need at that time to get the message.

I CAME FROM A LAND DOWN UNDER

On my return to England, I wasn't in a good place, financially or emotionally. Ever the optimist, I knew the fact I'd come from Australia with no debts and had no job to distract me from setting up Break-Point was a great blank canvas to work from. If I went straight into working for someone else because of the need to earn money, I would lose sight of my own goals. I had to start thinking about me. I even went for acupuncture to stop drinking. I wanted so badly to kick the booze because when I drank, I had no 'off' switch and before I knew it, I was losing four days at the back end of a three-day binge and it felt as if my life was going down the toilet. All my focus went into changing me, and to change my outer world, I had to change my inner one. I decided to exchange short-term pleasure for long-term discomfort.

There are three moments in my life where I've been saved from the brink of disaster. The first was the chimp attack, the next was when I was a juvenile delinquent and found myself in a remand home for two weeks, narrowly avoiding going to Borstal, and the third was in Iraq, when I was attacked by militia. Both the chimp attack and the attack in Iraq were times that I thought, 'That's it, this is your moment, you're going to die.'

One thing that these three events have in common was that none of them occurred during my time as a Special Forces soldier, whereas when these events happened, I was much more vulnerable and on my own. In the SBS, you're never alone, you've got so much support, all the weapons you need, all the tools – it's like being invincible. You can even call in an air-strike or naval gunfire from hundreds of miles away. And when you're part of a highly trained four-man team diving into targets underwater where there's no verbal communication, you're almost making decisions based on telepathy, it just flows.

However, break point is also about the small stuff. You don't need to welcome an attack by the militia or be attacked by a crazed animal to experience it. Once you learn to take care of the small stuff and allow this to be your modus operandi, the big stuff comes naturally. The way you do anything is how you do everything!

EXERCISE: SHORT-TERM DISCOMFORT

Make a note of at least three things today where you have stepped into the short-term discomfort for long-term gain. This can be as simple as cleaning the dishes before you head off to work, going for that run or doing daily exercise; making healthy food choices, or speaking out when you had a point. Any situation where you've felt uncomfortable but have just done it anyway, and it will have benefited you in the long term. Also make a note of when you could have done this and wish you had.

Three short-term discomforts

1. _____

2. _____

3. _____

When you could have experienced short-term discomfort

1. _____

2. _____

3. _____

In the above three cases, what would have happened if you had gone through the short-term discomfort?

1. _____

2. _____

3. _____

CHAPTER 6

GOALS

'A dream without a goal is merely an illusion.'

– Ollie Ollerton

One of the biggest questions people are asked when it comes to self-development is: 'Do you have any goals?' Well here's the thing, we all do! Your subconscious is a goal-striving mechanism which will stop at nothing until it's achieved your dominant thought topics. But be warned, if left unchecked your subconscious won't always select positive goals. Think about the football player running through on goal scared he's going to miss. His subconscious visualises and creates the negative outcome in the real world. It's far better to have goals that you desire as opposed to always achieving the things you hate. Think about that.

ROME WASN'T BUILT IN A DAY

Those who make plans and act on them are more likely to achieve what they want out of life, compared with those who meander with life's currents. When I returned from Australia I had one major goal and it was as clear in my mind as braille on fire: 'To create a globally recognised brand, recognised for the positive growth and development of others.'

Rome wasn't built in a day, there were teething problems with Break-Point. To start with I went into partnership with some people and it turned sour, caused the company a loss and I had to go the legal route to get rid of them. But the situation wasn't crushing, because my focus and end goal far overwhelmed it. It was a wrinkle not an earthquake. And looking back, at the time of starting up Break-Point I was still dealing with my demons, and they were getting in the way of progress. If you don't clear your mind as well as your life to be Battle Ready, you're going to be in survival mode dealing with emotional shit rather than focusing on your goal. In a state of stress we cannot be creative, and that spark of inner genius we all possess can never become a flame.

For those of you reading this who've had things go wrong with your own plans, refocus on what you are there to do, not just on the problem at hand, and remember that failure is an important foot servant of success. The more you fail, the stronger your finished success will be, because all those future pitfalls have already been made and dealt with en route! Refresh and reposition your energy. If the situation overwhelms you, and feels greater than your purpose, it's not the right purpose. When things get in the way, reinforce the positive affirmation of what you're focused on, and those past negatives won't slow you down. Your *purpose must outweigh your circumstances* otherwise you become a victim of your circumstances and will lose yourself in them, as well as losing sight of your path going forward. Remember, it doesn't take long for the grass to grow over a pathway.

Find the ignition you need to really propel yourself. Don't choose just any goal, but a *big* goal that when imagined, lights up your insides like a firework. No goal is ever great unless at some point you doubted your ability to achieve it. Some of us are born with our life's purpose staring straight back at us, like

Pablo Picasso who could draw before he could talk, and at seven years of age sat in most classes drawing a live pigeon he brought to school with him in his pocket. But while Picasso knew exactly what he wanted to do with his life from the word go, most of us are not like that and have to live through various experiences before we find what really nourishes our soul.

PROCESS

A dream without a plan is merely an illusion, because unless you have a plan to execute, your desire will always be just a thought. Yes, it's important to have imagination to start with, but at some stage you have to get your hands dirty and move into the action phase, and for this you need to apply a process, a system, a plan.

First of all, ask yourself, 'What do I want to achieve?' For example, it might be something like: 'I want to run a 20-mile race.' Instead of going straight out of the door, running 20 miles and doing yourself an injury, you create a plan by which you slowly increase your level of endurance, mile by mile. You start to create a process, for example: 'on Monday morning, I'm going to put my trainers on and walk out the door. I'm going to run a mile.' It needs some time specific detail, and it needs to be achievable.

Every great idea has a honeymoon period, and just thinking of it gives you a sense of euphoria. That said, unless the idea has a plan to realise it and you begin to move into the *doing* phase, it quickly withers on the vine. It's super important to disengage the mind and emotion, because your emotion will fall back into a repeat cycle of yesterday and tell you that you won't stick at your desired goal, what's the point of trying? The mind will create clever little games like telling you to go check your email, check your phone, or that there is something that really needs your attention; anything to make you procrastinate, to the point that you no longer have time to make a mark on the day and start the journey, the first footstep that takes you closer to where you want to be.

In order to actualise, you need to do something physically!

In the absence of clearly defined goals, we allow pointless trivia to consume our lives. Einstein once said: 'If you always do what you've always done, you'll always get what you've always got.' It's a question of energy and atoms, which is what we're all made of. Change the energy and the atoms will move themselves, but you need a clear plan of where you're heading.

YOU NEED A GOAL WITH A DATE

Once you have a goal with a date it will draw you towards its magnetic flux. You'll make decisions and take actions, each of which will be a building block, a step towards your realising your goal. And the more you plant the idea, the harder your subconscious will work, marshalling every fibre within you to get you there. It's not about being forever focused on the end goal, it's more that once you know where you're going, trust that it will happen and enjoy the journey. If it's a goal close to your heart it won't seem like hard work; rather, it will be a joy as you'll also be coming more of yourself, and the growth belittles the goal. We are on this planet as a mere blip in time and if you set your intention to the Universe without a realistic date in the near future, you may be looking at a good million years' time before it manifests itself!

10 REASONS WHY GOALS FAIL

- **It's not your goal** – You're doing it for someone else.
- **You have no emotional relationship with it** – Devotion requires emotion!
- **Your goal is boring** – You must be excited by your goal.
- **Your goal is greedy** – Focus on one goal at a time.
- **You haven't appreciated the obstacles** – Pre-warned is prepared.
- **Your future picture is not clear** – Clarity defies confusion.
- **You appreciate your limits over your goals** – Your limits become your reality.
- **Your goal doesn't know when it's due** – You must define a due date.
- **You didn't write and repeat daily** – Remain dynamic.
- **No plan survives first contact!** – Keep the goal, evolve the plan.

MAPPING THE TERRITORY

When you come up with a goal that excites you, it's vital you write it down. That helps create the seedling. Looking at the big picture, what's your first step going to be? You need to get to know the landscape around your goal and do some investigating. While your overarching goal might be 'I'm going to run a successful five-star restaurant', that's too big a leap coming from nothing and you're setting yourself up for a punishing failure that will knock your confidence. What you can do though is begin reading about people who started restaurants, the challenges they faced and how they resolved them, lifehacks, tips from those who have been through it already. Forewarned is forearmed, isn't it? In making your own initial investigations you will slowly build your confidence and knowledge, finessing your vision until the point that you're ready to go ahead. You can't do anything without knowledge, so start making it real. Do your due diligence and mental mapping. And, just like with the Mission Success Cycle (see page 160), plan for what obstacles might come up, both external and internal.

BREAKING YOUR GOAL DOWN

When setting up Break-Point, I made sure my goal was broken down into bitesize chunks I could tackle: I looked at creating the website and constructing the programmes and course agenda that allowed me to visualise as I put them together. I set dates of when we would have our first corporate and public offerings, and figures of what I would be earning per month. I considered the cost of the equipment we'd need to run the course, should we buy it on HP or rent it?

Setting positive and realistic goals is crucially important. If your goal is overwhelming, and it should be, break it down into manageable steps. Short, medium and long-term goals. Choose goals that mean something to you, not what someone else expects of you. Remember Bruce Lee, confined to his bed unable to walk, placing affirmations around his room so he never stopped visualising walking again? Write down your goal, take a photo of it so it's on your phone, on your screensaver, on the fridge. Or if you're a person that responds more to images than words, make a vision board with pictures. Wherever you go, repeat the goal to yourself under your breath. If you want to make a lifestyle change and create a better you, then you must focus purely upon that goal.

Now my goal was a big one, creating a globally recognised brand from nothing. I still haven't achieved this yet! But anyone hearing it would have said I was off my head. In order that I didn't feel overwhelmed to the point of abandoning it in favour of something easier, I stopped looking at the bigger picture and broke it down into digestible sections. The easiest way to climb a mountain is not looking at that menacing faraway peak and thinking, 'Shit, I'll never have the energy to go all that way, it's too daunting.' Instead, it's about putting one foot in front of the other and having waypoints to head to, camps en route where you can catch your breath. It's about getting your head down, taking your eye off the prize and digging in.

And instead of looking up at the mountain, take the time to look *back* and see how far you've come, how well you have done, it's an amazing view! Before you know it, you're halfway, then three-quarters of the climb and soon enough you'll be riding that bad boy like a rocking horse!

EXERCISE: BREAKING DOWN
THE GOAL AND CREATING A SMART GOAL

Think of your goal. What are the stages you need to break it down in order to make it happen? Create a timeline for each stage. You could use the clock method mentioned earlier.

_____

_____

_____

_____

_____

_____

_____

_____

_____

_____

_____

_____

_____

_____

_____

_____

_____

_____

Now try to make your goal SMART. SMART stands for the following:

Is your goal **specific** enough?
How will you **measure** its success?
Is it **achievable**?
Is it **relevant** towards your greater goal?
Does it have a **timeframe**?
Apply the SMART framework to your goal:

_____

_____

_____

_____

_____

_____

_____

_____

_____

_____

THE JOURNEY OVERWHELMS THE GOAL

When you achieve your goal, remember that all those milestones you reached and mistakes you made were all part of the journey. Churchill once said, 'Success is the ability to bounce enthusiastically from one failure to the next.' If it was smooth running all the way, it wasn't a big enough goal. Be proud that you kept going and fought through the obstacles, the learning, negativity and mind telling you it was pointless.

Once you get to the goal the journey overwhelms it. In other words, all the experience and wisdom you've experienced on your journey is so much more than the goal itself. Once there, do we rest on our laurels and return to sloth? No, the human brain and body thrive on new challenges. We need to constantly draw up new goals and fill our days with a sense of achievement. Achievement begets confidence and self-belief.

Often you could be halfway through achieving your goal when you find yourself suddenly compelled to create another. For instance, somebody whose goal is to go back to college and get a degree might find the self-respect they were looking for and then go off and do something else more fulfilling. People are muddling through life like it's an endurance test, earning enough money to pay for the house, the mortgage and the finance on their cars. There must be more.

RUN THROUGH THE FINISH LINE

Many of us fail at the point of success. For some it's because we don't feel we're worthy of the achievement, for others because of the stress and the pressure we place on ourselves. It's the moment when you feel yourself veering towards the negative, when you self-sabotage and allow the voice of doubt to start talking you out of it; instead of encouraging you to dig deeper, your mind is telling you to take the shortcut and end the stress. Regarding evolution, you are now starting to threaten the species – this is the survival blueprint in full flare! In this moment, Breathe – Recalibrate – Deliver.

Breathe – Deep breaths and focus on what you want to achieve (lower cortisol levels)

Recalibrate – Disengage emotion and feelings that are not serving you

Deliver – Take positive action towards your goal

The process above should take no more than five seconds. While on missions we understood the risk when we hit our targets and eliminated the threat, for at this point we were more aware than ever of the possibility of counter-attack, and mission failure was highly likely; hence our focus went *beyond* the goal and didn't rest on it.

CHAPTER 7

THE ROLE OF VISUALISATION

My head is always full of pictures and possible scenarios. If I was a Mr Men character, I would be Mr Daydream. Since I was a kid, I've had this ability to allow my mind to wander and vividly imagine things happening to me and others. On many occasions they have turned out exactly as I imagined. At first it was troubling, now I find it reassuring as it proves, at least to me, that we are more in charge of our destiny than we give ourselves credit for.

One of the first times this happened was back in Staffordshire in the eighties. The matter concerned a girl who was well known as a spiteful bully from a bad local family. She grassed me up for having a sawn-off shotgun, which though I concede was the case, landed me in a police cell for the weekend. I kept idly thinking how I would like to get my revenge on her, and on my release, I was bombing down a very long steep hill lost in my daydreams and not really concentrating when I ran straight into her at full speed at the bottom of the hill. She appeared from nowhere, as if I had willed it. Let's face it, she could have been anywhere else in the town, she *just happened* to be in that exact place at the second I was flying past. I felt like Damien Thorn from *The Omen*!

I fully believe that our lives are a product of what goes on in our heads. If your life is a mess, it's because you accept those thoughts in your head. You and only you can change the colour of those thoughts.

I've always been an optimist; I could find a silver lining in a mushroom cloud. People who know me often remark that no matter how bad a situation I've got myself into, I always seem to come up smelling of roses. I flip bad situations into better ones just by focusing on what good has come from that situation. It may be slim pickings at times but from every circumstance there comes an opportunity. I analyse exactly what's happened and I always find something good in every situation, so that's exactly where my focus is. I always say to myself: 'It could have been a lot worse.' Having a positive mindset is half the battle in life and allows you to take risks others wouldn't touch with a bargepole. It's also a case of trusting that the solutions are within you no matter how bad the shitstorm gets. You have to triage the problem: ask yourself, 'What can I control in the chaos?' If you have a growth mindset rather than a shut-down negative one, you'll always find a way out.

A major component of optimism is the ability to visualise something good happening, to see it in diamond-clear detail and to be able to place yourself in that imaginary scenario and feel how you would feel if it was real. Visualisation is so powerful that it can be dangerous if not directed consciously, which is why people who build negative future scenarios in their minds usually get what they ask for. We're quite happy to sit and worry for hours and days about something we don't want, so why don't we change that to something we do want? The more you practise it, the more it delivers and so on …

BUBBLES & BULLETS

In 2003, a few months after the overthrow of Saddam Hussein, I was in post-war Iraq working security for ABC News, ferrying journos across Baghdad and beyond. It was tense and bombs were still going off but there was hope the worst was over. News companies started cutting the level of their security protection and I found myself team-leading an operation to pick up a very precious 'package' – the new ABC bureau chief – from Jordan on a 28-hour round trip. Part of his job was to assess the need for the rather expensive security detail he had hired (i.e., us). What should have been at least six of us ensuring the safety of him and his team of eleven was shaved down to myself and one other operative, Dave. It was a crazy situation to be placed in, but we desperately wanted to hold on to the contract with the news company, so we agreed to cut corners, which is what you did in the absence of the awe and might of military tools and protocol.

Up to this point in my life I'd been pretty good at visualising – it had got me into the Royal Marines and the SBS. Without realising what I was doing, I had focused on how getting accepted by them would make me feel, how it would affect my life, and how it would affect those people around me when I passed. I hung on to the desire for that outcome and felt the emotions around it. I used all my senses to evoke it: touch, smell, feel, hearing, taste. I placed myself in the situation of passing Selection, imagining the people who really mattered to me. I felt their warm hands closing about my own and shaking my hand. Visualisation comes naturally to me; I am more of a creative person than an analytical one, so I'm somewhat of an expert when it comes to painting pictures in my mind. Attaching a layer of emotion to these pictures makes them feel real.

There's more to just *wanting* something though, you've got to resonate with it and experience an emotional reaction. And if it doesn't spark genuine excitement in you when you picture it then it's worthless to you, it *must* resonate. You can't expect to just say a few words that don't attach to an emotion, it's about creating a visual picture of where you want to be, how it's going to benefit you, how it will feel. If you create that emotional state around your desired outcome, it causes a chemical reaction within the body that pulls you towards the direction of where you imagine you're going to be.

Dave and I drove for 14 hours to Amman. We were to spend the night at the Intercontinental Hotel before picking up 'the package' the following morning. During that journey I had a long time to think, and what better to focus my thoughts on but the opposite of what seemed to be imminent. I thought about how it would feel to keep this contract for eternity and how already my financial circumstances had changed dramatically. How would that richness affect my life? What could I use my money for? How could it benefit me and the other people around me? I painted pictures in my mind so large that I ran out of mental canvas. I then targeted my thoughts on the journey that would take me to this goal, for unless something monumental happened, there was no way that we could influence the ABC bureau chief through mere charming conversation. My thoughts ran away and went into specific detail about what would happen the very next day. I didn't truly believe at that point I was changing my destiny, but simply letting my foot off the brake on my over-creative imagination.

That evening I sat at the bar with Dave and discussed the possible and likely imminent loss of the contract with ABC. I bought us both a beer and allowed him to get halfway down the glass before presenting him with my thoughts.

'Listen, mate,' I said to him. 'This contract cannot end. You know what needs to happen, don't you? The only way we're going to keep this contract? We need to be attacked!'

Dave looked at me with a rather confused expression on his face, like I was a madman.

I repeated myself. 'Mate, we need to be attacked!' I bought him another beer before I delivered the detail of my statement.

'So, this is what's going to happen. We're going to leave here, pick up the 12 of them and drive them over the border. Then somewhere between Ramadi and Fallujah we're going to be attacked by the militia—'

'What!?' said Dave.

'We're going to be attacked but we'll get the ABC people out of the fire-fight, and when we get to Baghdad there's going to be a heroes' welcome. And, when the champagne's been popped, the bureau chief is going to sign a new contract on the spot.'

I relayed it all to Dave in forensic detail – how I could imagine the smell of the cordite from the bullets in the shots we'd exchange, arriving at the final destination unscathed … tasting the champagne and feeling the bubbles tickling my nose, the coldness of the glass in my hand, and that I could see the gratitude in the bureau chief's face, feel the grip of his handshake. Once I painted the picture, I spent the rest of the night going through the scenario in my head. I placed myself at the start and ran through the complete event as if I was there.

I woke early the next morning and collected the 'package' and his entourage. We were the rear vehicle of a four-car convoy responsible for the protection and safety of all vehicles in front. Our low-profile, soft-skin (as in, bullets go through) Toyota Land Cruisers rolled out of the hotel compound. We made it to the border, which as always was a hideous and time-consuming event. Once out the other side we went to find our cache in the middle of the desert which contained our weapons and ammunition. We then set off on our monster of a return trip back to Baghdad.

Minutes blended into hours as the infinity of parched desert, punctuated only by the odd camel, reeled by outside our windows.

There was no sign of any other vehicles. Ten hours into the drive it was my turn to take the wheel, a small MP5 KURZ sub-machine gun lay across my lap ready for any unwanted encounters. At least we'd broken the back of this horrendous journey; I couldn't wait to get to our destination. But I was tired; the combo of yesterday's and today's long drive, mixed with the adrenalin of being on constant alert finally took its toll and I fell asleep for a second, coming to as we passed a sign reading 'Ramadi'. We were driving on a three-lane highway, hard and close to the central reservation at around 100kph. I noticed a sign in the dusk light to my left that said 'Fallujah' and as my eyes glanced at my rear-view mirror, I noticed the deliberate flashing of headlights in the distance. I immediately informed my number two and he identified the vehicle was moving fast and marked another vehicle further behind it. They were getting close, fast.

My mind immediately focused on everything I didn't want it to be, as I made assumptions of what it could be: 'Was it the Americans?' Suddenly – in two vehicles with windows dark as midnight – they became sufficiently close enough for me to realise it wasn't the Americans. I immediately moved on to my next assumption: 'Is it another security company?'

I started to think I'd best get onto my comms and move the convoy over to the right of the three-way to let them past, for by this moment they were pretty much on our bumper. Then all the windows in the vehicle were sliding down. Immediately the Arab headdress gave it away, as I realised this was my worst-nightmare scenario of 'being attacked' that I'd sugar-coated the day before as being my perfect dream.

I informed the convoy in front and gave the order to increase speed. It was at that point I also realised we were at the exact spot that I had described us being attacked the night before in the bar – somewhere between Ramadi and Fallujah. 'You idiot!' I told myself, 'What have you done?' For this is exactly what I had predicted to Dave would happen. It felt so familiar it was like an out of body experience.

The car sped after us, engine roaring, our speedometer touching 130kph as it caught us. A second wave of panic took a grip of me as I saw AK47s appear from every window, followed by the intimidating orchestra of bullets screaming over our vehicle. I was in a state of panic, a state of shock, but the sound of the AKs' barking snapped me into operator mode and that's when my training kicked in.

Breathe – Relax and be conscious of your breathing
Recalibrate – Triage the situation to one to two things that you can control
Deliver – Take appropriate action based on clarity of thought

This was taking a step into the discomfort of the unknown for any chance of long-term gain – that's to say, my ultimate survival.

This was break point – kill or be killed.

Short-term comfort would have been to comply to the demands of the attackers, which would have inevitably led to long-term discomfort, in this case, death.

I aggressively swung our car over to the right and matched their speed to close in towards my number-three vehicle and block them in. They sped up to fill the gap. With one of our cars in front of them, the central reservation to their immediate left, and my car to the right of them, they had fallen for my trap and were now boxed in. I looked down to my left and the world had slowed down to such a pace I felt like I'd forgotten to breathe. I was now in flow state, this was peace in war. With the militia's AK47s poking directly at us, their faces obscured by *shimags* (headscarves), I was so close I could see the whites of their eyes. The one nearest me was barely a teen.

A millisecond passed between us. He looked at me and I back at him, my finger sliding into the trigger housing of my sub-machine gun, my face flat without emotion. It was a break point – act or be killed. Time to debug: Breathe, Recalibrate and Deliver. I gave Dave the order to open fire, as I lifted my weapon to rest on my left arm commanding the steering wheel. Our first few rounds cleared the glass of our closed windows as we emptied a salvo of bullets onto the attackers.

I tasted cordite, heard the report of the guns echoing in my ears as hot air flew in the shattered window, the enemy vehicle slowing to a halt in the rear view, a plume of black smoke rising from its bonnet. Its support vehicle stopped but didn't follow us. We drove on through the burning afternoon toward Baghdad, my ears ringing from the confined space of the attack. All the while I kept thinking: 'What the fuck just happened!?' I was genuinely freaked out by how accurate the real event was with my visualised version. I'd been so close to death, but had I really ordered that? I took no pleasure or glory in shooting the youth. I radioed ahead to alert the base that we'd come under fire but had prevailed. There were protocols to observe. You couldn't just take a life, it had to stand up to some rigorous criteria before it could be deemed as lawful and in self-defence.

When we arrived back at the compound, the doors flew open and we were immediately greeted by the welcome party … of course! I opened the Land Cruiser's door and a shower of shattered glass and spent rounds tinkled out on the floor, catching my attention. But as I looked up amid the noise of people clapping our return, someone handed me a glass of champagne. This was crazy. I glanced at Dave; he was looking at me like I was some kind of witch.

Shortly after our arrival, we were summoned by the bureau chief who vigorously shook my hand with a look of gratitude and commended us for our actions. He was in the vehicle in front or ours and had seen the whole thing. He then slid a piece of paper across the table and I signed the contract for an immediate extension of our services. It was just as I had imagined it, so much so that it felt like déjà vu.

Much more than another two years of guaranteed income, this experience was a defining and spiritual moment for me, as if the Universe had given me a glimpse of what could be achieved with a little willpower and persistence: visualise something with enough clarity and detail and it will happen. It also scared the shit out of me regarding how careful we have to be with our thoughts. I vowed never again to wish an attack on myself; it just might happen.

There is something to be said about almost being killed, it tends to wake you up, sharpen your senses, you gain a heightened self-awareness. I realised that night how careful I needed to be in what I wished for, and just how powerful a tool visualisation could be in my future life.

Thinking negatively attracts exactly what you fear. But once you are passionate about your purpose and acting on your intention, you're no longer in a state of fear, or loss. Instead you're in harmony with your flow. Buddhists call needing something material or feeling the world owes you a living a state of lack. A need suggests a dependency as opposed to a desire, which is a want. It's important to understand the difference because you shouldn't be doing anything out of need. So 'I want this to happen' or 'This will happen' will invite positive results. Needing something is the ego's language.

That's why many relationships fail, because the balance is lost as soon as one person develops the *need*. Dependency. To their surprise, people who moan about their jobs often find themselves being made redundant or the company they work for folds, because their envisioning has created a negative vibration and they get what they've been asking for. Then they say, 'I knew that would happen!'

As we'll see in Chapter 11, when it came to envisioning the birth and success of my company, I went into minute detail, visualising exactly how it would look and how I would feel. I had already begun this process during my epiphany while flying over the Outback while working for the oil company, when I saw in perfect clarity the uniforms of my staff and the corporate participants on our training course. The success I focused on with such detail and conviction soon resulted in the phone call from my friend Foxy to tell me about the opportunity of a new series called *SAS: Who Dares Wins*. Setting up the company when the series was released was such a golden opportunity, as it provided a brilliant launchpad to give Break-Point the PR wings it needed to fly.

EXERCISE: VISUALISATION

Here are two exercises. Try the first before you attempt the second:

1. Imagine you've got a million pounds. Picture it inside a bank vault, the cash piled up in a neat block of pristine £50 notes tightly wrapped in plastic.

2. This time imagine the experiences and the things you could do for yourself and other people if you had a million pounds to play with. Imagine buying a dream house, your favourite car, or taking your parents or loved ones on the trip of a lifetime, seeing their faces smiling, tears of happiness in their eyes; maybe it's a charity you'd like to give the money to and make a real difference.

What did you notice about the two different visualisations? Hopefully, the first left you cold and lacked depth, while the second gave you a positive emotion. It's that emotion you need to engage with. You've got to have the vibration that matches the desire. When you don't have that vibration it's worthless.

CHAPTER 8

CREATING POSITIVE BEHAVIOURS

BATTLE READY

Being Battle Ready is more than just a state of mind, it's a sense of being ready for anything that hits the fan and making sure that everything in your life is squared away, eliminating the Shortcut Syndrome and not cutting corners. When you're Battle Ready, you don't defer dealing with shit that can hurt you. Why put off till tomorrow what you can do today?

When we plan an operation in the Special Forces, we think of any possible curveball that might be thrown at us, we sweat the small stuff, the minutiae, so when things go south, we have a contingency plan. You plan and you breathe. When you come to the big execution, if you haven't done the planning properly then you're carrying through stuff that's going to affect what you need to do. It's about being ready for anything, so that when something surfaces that's unpredicted, you have the bandwidth and the ability to deal with it, not leaving stuff unactioned, letters unopened for weeks etc. We only have a short window of opportunity. If you don't react to your impulses, your brain will talk you out of it. Our brains are wired to avoid stress, although if you continually do that in the short term, the long term effects are far more severe.

When you make too many shortcuts life becomes mayhem, and because you're not dealing with it, it fogs the clarity of your purpose. When you think of an idea you must act on it, even if it doesn't suit your circumstances right now. I know that if I don't action something immediately, because my life is so busy, it'll get left to one side and it'll be another thing that is not squared away. Especially with my business, if an idea pops up in my head, I'll send the email or make the call to whoever I need to help get the ball rolling right away. Then I've offloaded it, it's hit the other person, and it will come back to me. Action creates reaction. I've dealt with it instead of saying, 'Yeah, that's a good idea, I'll do it later ...'

Regardless of how small it might be, you must take an action, as that will cause a reaction from someone else. Ideas are worthless unless you make them physical and tangible. I hear so many people saying, 'I thought of that', and I say to them, 'But you never took any action on it.' It's much easier to claim the idea, than to action it.

Actualising my ideas only happened later in life because previously I was dealing with so much stress. Before I woke up I was so consumed by my financial and emotional situations that I didn't have the bandwidth to deal with anything creative. In odd moments of clarity I would think, 'That would be a good idea', but before you could say 'prevarication', I would be sucked into the issues of the day, too busy earning a living to think about anything else. When you're Battle Ready, your home life is organised, your relationships are balanced and squared away so that you can start releasing your true potential. It's about facing up to your finances, ensuring you've got something put away for a rainy day. That's when you have the bandwidth and clarity to create. Stress and instability mustn't affect your plans.

I don't go to work in the morning and distract myself with chatter like, 'Oh shit, my relationship with my girlfriend Laura is in trouble … I said this, and she said that.' If domestic trouble is a constant in your life, then you need to either resolve it or if it's a damaging relationship then you need to think about whether it is in both of your best interests to continue. Does it provide you with more positives than negatives and give you more energy than it takes away? While you're in a mindset of stress and instability you'll never be creating, you'll never achieve anything much. Fortunately for me, in my current relationship, I'm 100 per cent supported, so I don't need to waste time worrying.

Our minds were meant to be creative, but we spend so much time in the survival default mode, worrying and obsessing with what has happened in our lives, what isn't happening and fretting about the future, that the delicate seedling of our ideas gets choked before it's even made it to the page.

CREATING POSITIVE BEHAVIOURS

'The quality of our lives depends on the quality of our habits.'
– James Clear, Atomic Habits

Forty per cent of an average person's daily actions are based on habits that happen automatically, as if they're sleepwalking, while the remaining 60 per cent are governed consciously. The brain looks for shortcuts and ways to be lazy, so anything that we repeat on a regular basis soon becomes assumed as a habit, be it driving a car, running in the morning, playing an instrument or speaking a new language, and the brain then allows itself to relax once again and switch off.

So let's consider some typical behaviours many of us would like to change, bad habits if you will: smoking, opening a bottle of wine the same time every evening, losing our temper, eating too much fried food, hitting 'snooze' and sleeping in, or leaving things till the last minute: even if they are lazy they are all learned behaviour. The good news is you can unload these unhelpful behaviours and create positive new habits in their place in a very short space of time. However, if these new traits are to become embedded as routine, they demand self-discipline and a keenness of intent from you. Building a better version of yourself starts through building those habits until they become second nature.

If you're having trouble changing your habits, the problem isn't you, the problem is your system. Bad habits repeat themselves again and again not because you don't want to change, but because you have the wrong system for change. We don't rise to the level of our goals; we fall to the level of our processes. Creating new habits takes an enormous amount of discipline for you to have any chance of making a change that lasts for good. In the beginning, if you don't plan sufficiently and are not focused on the goal 100 per cent, you'll hit a minefield of distractions that attempt to pull you back into your comfort zone of safety – the no-growth zone!

Ensure you make a plan and stick rigidly to it. I have to implement this whenever I try to change the patterns of the past or when I've simply fallen off track and need to refocus. Always have the goal in your mind and whenever that devious thought pattern comes to play, ask yourself, 'Does that thinking take me towards my goal or not?' If 'not' then you must either wipe that thought from your mind or go straight over the obstacle that sits right in front of you.

Remember the order of this trinity: Trigger, Behaviour, Reward.

This is the way habits work: the trigger sparks the behaviour, which then delivers the reward or, if it's a bad habit, 'the consequence', as bad habits work the same way. When you're starting a positive habit or kicking a negative habit think of what the triggers are that lead to the behaviour.

'If you don't like where you are, make your today a tomorrow to be proud of.'

– Ollie Ollerton

EXERCISE: HABIT FORMATION

Imagine a positive goal, like running a marathon in six months' time.

Trigger: Stick your workout programme on the fridge. If you're planning on running first thing in the morning and you're a bit of a sleepy dormouse come 6 a.m., place your kit and trainers right by the bed so when your alarm goes, they are the first thing you see. Use your phone as the alarm and put it outside the door so you must get up to turn it off. Do not go back to bed!

BREATHE – RECALIBRATE – DELIVER

Behaviour: Go to the gym/run.

Reward: Feel satisfied with yourself, look healthier, see your mileage getting higher and your fitness level improving. Tell yourself how amazing you are! Feel the positive endorphins flow.

If it's a bad habit you want to change, for example, kicking smoking:

Trigger: Don't keep cigarettes in the house. If you've always associated drinking alcohol with your cigarette, avoid drinking alcohol in the first few weeks of stopping. Don't hang out with friends who are smokers in the first days or weeks of stopping. When you 'feel' the urge, fall into process.

BREATHE – RECALIBRATE – DELIVER

Behaviour: Make it difficult for yourself to access cigarettes by walking a different route to work so you don't pass the shop where you usually buy them. Become more Battle Ready by saving the money you would have spent on cigarettes, putting it into a savings account or on a gym membership.

Reward: Feel proud of yourself, enjoy fresher breath, looking healthier, feeling fitter.

If you fall off the healthy wagon and back into smoking, don't be too hard on yourself. Think about what other triggers might have been at work to make you reach for the cigarettes – did you miss any? Add them to your list and think of any new behaviours to help deal with these new triggers. Remember the negatives smoking brings to your life, how expensive it is these days, not to mention your increased chances of developing lung cancer and the drain on the health system.

Think back to the Purpose Pyramid: ask yourself,' What is the purpose of smoking?' Unless the pros outweigh the cons, reset and start again remembering all the benefits you'll enjoy when you've given up. Statistics prove that asking these questions while conducting the negative habit will produce an increased chance of quitting. So, while you're puffing on your cigarette ask the question while understanding the benefits of the smell and taste.

Creating habits: Think of one good habit you are trying to promote, and one bad habit you are trying to kick. What are the triggers? What behaviour can you bring in to help you change? What is the reward?

Good habit:

_____

What are the triggers?

_____

_____

_____

What behaviour will effect change?

_____

_____

_____

What is the reward?

_____

_____

_____

Bad habit:

_____

What are the triggers?

_____

_____

_____

What behaviour will effect change?

_____

_____

_____

What is the reward?

_____

_____

_____

If you go back into bad habits or don't establish your good ones, there's no point in bemoaning your lack of willpower or berating yourself, it just makes you feel like crap and affects your morale, which will make you fall back into your bad habits. Have some compassion for yourself, appreciate what you're doing is hard and that it is normal to have the odd failure and relapse on the way to creating a new habit. But conversely, don't be too soft on yourself either. Studies show that people who cut themselves a little slack when they relapse are more likely to jump back into the challenge than those who get lost in self-loathing. Remember you will attract exactly what your dominant thoughts are.

THE THOUGHT FARM

Imagine moving towards your desired goal as being like a rice farmer growing his crop. First, he ploughs the soil, removing any weeds that might limit future growth. Similarly, to create the best mental environment possible for your idea to flourish, your mind must be cleared of unnecessary distractions, anything outstanding or bothering it, so you can fully focus on the task.

Next, the seedling is buried underwater in the mud, just as the visualisation of our idea is planted into our mind and subconscious.

A rice farmer sleeps close to his crop in a shaded hut to protect him from the sun. Like the farmer, don't risk over-exposing your goal to others. It's easy talking about it but there comes a point where action speaks louder than words.

Throughout its growth the rice is vulnerable to bugs and birds. Throughout the lifespan of growing your goal, water it with positivity, clear processes and positive habits; it's at its early stages of growth that it's most vulnerable; people may tell you your goal is too difficult/not needed/been tried before, or you may be plagued by negative memories of previous failures, which further your self-doubt. The Mind will tell you anything to keep you in your familiar comfort zone. Can we get rid of these negative memories for good? Only if we stop holding on to the past and dwelling in our comfort zones; only if we stop projecting into the future and start living in the now.

Every farm has waste and weeds and we must ensure these are regularly cleared otherwise they will affect the new and positive crops coming to bear. You must also invest in waste management and ensure that the rotting crops are kept in an area that does not risk any contamination to the new and flourishing fresh crops. If contained properly they will actually produce good compost which when broken down will offer assistance in the growth of new crops. Even rotten old crops have something good to offer when it comes to the birth of something new.

The farmer is guided by the timeline of the seasons, planting his seedlings during the monsoon season when there is an abundance of rain. Planning is everything; too early or too late could render the idea worthless. When is the best time to realise our goal?

MISSION SUCCESS CYCLE

The Mission Success Cycle is a tool similar to what we used in the Special Forces as an easy but effective means of ensuring each mission follows a process that gives it every chance of success with minimal casualties. It's designed to follow a process as opposed to opinion and feelings, and ensure that regardless of what's going on in your head, you have a systematic routine to follow to get you where you want to be while maintaining momentum. It helps deal with a large amount of complex info in a very digestible, time-efficient manner. And I can verify it works like a treat. How? I'm still breathing! It is also transferrable to pretty much any situation you can imagine, not just hostage rescues and drug raids. It can also be used in team meetings, putting on a rave, setting up a safari in your back garden … Okay, now I'm being silly but you get my drift. It can be as simple or complex as you wish.

There are four parts to the process.

Plan – Look at all assets and resources available. Is there any intelligence based on past operations or on new information from current intelligence sources? The question is, 'What do you have to play with, and what's for and against us?' Ask yourself the following questions:

- What is your objective?
- What are you looking to achieve?
- When are you looking to achieve it?
- What are the potential threats or obstacles that might stand in your way?
- What capabilities have you got to deal with these?
- What are your physical, financial and intellectual assets and how can you best use them towards your goal?
- Do you have any relevant experience that you can draw on? If so, what worked and what didn't in the past?
- Who in your team will be best suited to execute different stages of the plan?

Brief – All four aspects of the MSC are equally important to the Special Forces during operations but success stemmed mainly from the Briefing Phase. The brief is the delivery of the mission, verbalised using the information taken from the plan. This is a walk-through of the mission in slow time and a time for anyone to voice any concerns as to why it won't work or indeed anything that can increase chances of success. It's when you check your kit while the instructions are delivered in a clear and succinct fashion. It's also when any internal conflicts among the team can be ironed out, or any possible confusion sorted so when the real event happens there is no procrastination. Everybody involved has to be present so each of you knows exactly who is where and doing what at any given time during the delivery. Make sure you are prepared for worse-case scenarios.

Delivery – Provided the plan and the brief have been done correctly and all people involved in the delivery have contributed, the delivery should be seamless! But remember 'No plan survives first contact!' or, as Mike Tyson said, 'Everyone has a plan, until they get punched in the face!' When it gets noisy everything can change. However, providing your plan and brief are done correctly, you will have enough bandwidth to deal with contingency planning. This is in effect the ethos underlying the concept of being Battle Ready. If you're in a shit state when the shit hits the fan, there's a lot of shit flying around! This will fracture your efforts to counter any unplanned events, taking you off course.

Debrief – the Mission Success Cycle is not just about having a brief before your crucial meeting/event/challenge, it's also about following it up straight afterwards, while it's still fresh, so you can identify what wasn't working and what can be finessed.

Unlike in the business world where teams and companies don't make time to capture the learning points after a project has been completed, in the Special Forces we would go into a 'hot' debrief straight from the theatre of engagement, no matter the hour. It gave us the chance to learn and improve, regardless of whether the mission had been a success or not, and was an open environment where any of the team could say: 'Yeah, Ollie could have covered the other door when we breached the compound.' And someone else might say, 'Yeah, well, Foxy did really well by covering that for him.' the debrief is rank-less and a good team is made up of individuals that welcome positive as well as negative feedback.

In the Special Forces you're grown-ups, you don't have egos getting in the way when lives are on the line. You also develop trust. So, I suppose, 360-degree feedback (judgement from everyone around you, not just those in command) is not a difficult thing if your life or someone else's might depend on it. Once you create that environment of honesty, this is where you learn; you achieve growth through the advice of others.

Make sure that any key info gathered from the debrief is shared among the whole team as just one piece of information might affect all of them. Keep a record of what worked and what didn't to save time and energy for future projects. The Mission Success Cycle is a brilliant tool for its thoroughness, simplicity and transparency.

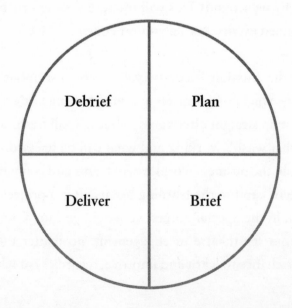

EXERCISE: MISSION SUCCESS

Think of an objective that you'd like to achieve.

Objective:

_____

_____

Plan:

_____

_____

_____

_____

Brief:

_____

_____

_____

_____

Deliver:

_____

_____

_____

_____

Debrief:

_____

_____

_____

_____

Once you've achieved Mission Success, learn to create a process where you learn and grow from every experience both good and bad. By doing this, you don't have to recreate the wheel every time a new project or opportunity is presented to you.

CHOOSING THE RIGHT TRIBE

Success in life comes down to many factors, one of which is the kind of people you have around you. Do they inspire you, or encourage you to do things that are bad for you? A positive and trusted sponsor, friend or mentor goes a long way in helping you achieve your purpose and can spur you on at those low times when you question your ability and your goal seems a long way away from being achieved. Similarly, at these times when you're vulnerable it can take just a few negative comments from the wrong person to make you doubt yourself and send you scurrying back to your comfort zone.

There are also people who do want you to succeed, positive people who will inspire and support your every move. But, unfortunately, there are also people who don't want you to succeed because they feel threatened by your success, or perhaps they are projecting their own fears on to you. There are the needy energy vampires, the false friends full of *schadenfreude* who relish things being bad for their friends, and there's those who dampen your self-belief with their negativity. Should you tolerate someone who questions your ability and rubbishes your goal? Faced with the option of having a negative friend or none at all, I'd go for the latter. It's better to keep your own counsel and spur yourself on rather than have someone else transfer their baggage on to you. I think a major part of success in life is learning to navigate around people you need to avoid.

When starting out on something new and intrepid (remember the seedling with the rice farmer), it's important to protect your idea. Often it will be someone in your family or a close friend who knocks you off course. And while they may not be intentionally trying to stop you achieving and are just trying to defend you from what might go wrong, they can be the most damaging, as we trust and listen to them the most.

When making changes to your life you must choose your tribe carefully. You need like-minded positive types who are going to support your journey, not take you off course. Aristotle, the fourth century BC philosopher, once suggested there are three kinds of friends in life: the familial – a blood tie that binds you but doesn't necessarily blossom into real friendship; the utility friendship – work colleagues with whom you share a common goal, a bit of banter but wouldn't trust your deepest fears with; and finally the close friend – those people you choose as an extension of yourself, reflecting your values and interests. What makes them special is a chemical reaction of mutual connection; they just seem to get us and all our idiosyncrasies, and we them. Time is precious, a commodity most of us have less of than we need, so it's important not to carry people who are not good for us, or who drain or diminish us. Positivity breeds positivity.

As we grow up, we realise it becomes less important to have loads of friends and more important to have *real* friends. The success of friendship is based on a healthy two-way street of give and take. If you were to conduct a cursory audit of all the current colleagues and friends in your life along the criteria of how supportive they are, how happy they make you feel, how loyal they are, and how much give and take there is in your relationship, how would your balance sheet look? Certain relationships will probably have grown lazy or lost their shine because you've both gravitated to different things and have lost the common thread that once held you together. Like the energy of money passing from one person to the next, the people in your life are also a fluid thing and relationships always need to be maintained in order to thrive. But the older the friendship the harder it is to be objective about what you get from one another; after all, you've been friends so long and shared so much history you can't imagine not having that shared memory resource any longer. Past experiences bind you together, true, but a relationship should continue to grow organically, not rely on things that happened decades ago.

The state of our friendships and the way others treat us reflects how we view ourselves; a person of low self-worth will allow themselves to be surrounded by people who are negative and think little of them. An addict will seek other addicts. A bully will seek weak people who will support his actions.

When we think about it objectively, how many of our friends are good for us, and how many are not? Gradually as we age, insubstantial relationships fall away, as circumstances move us in new social circles or perhaps to different countries, and individuals get left behind. I left for distant shores in 2003 and returned eleven years later. My good friends like Foxy were still there and meeting them was like I hadn't been away. It was a natural culling and I lost a fair few friends but in turn had more time for the ones that deserved my investment and gave me an ROI. That's life. If we're lucky, after all of life's vagaries, we're left with a pool of people with whom we share our troubles and joys, hopes and disappointments. The law of attraction suggests that it's only when we make a change and create a vacuum that it is filled with something new. And yet sentimentalists that we are, we tend to hold on to toxic relationships which are draining.

EXERCISE: WHO'S IN MY TRIBE?

On a separate sheet of paper compile a list of the people you speak to most on a weekly basis. For each person ask the following questions:

- Do they ask me about myself?
- Do I trust them?
- Is our friendship/working relationship a two-way street?
- Are they dependable?
- Do they suck or radiate energy?
- Are they control freaks?
- How do you feel when you see their name calling on your phone?

When you tally up if there are more negatives than positives then you know if it is a fair relationship.

BUDDYING UP

A great friend is worth their weight in gold. Consider the people you respect and trust and ask yourself if they might be prepared to help you achieve your goal, and how you can repay them. Do they have something they too want to attempt? Could you check in regularly on each other's progress, coach one another? In the Special Forces someone always had my back and I always had theirs.

When it comes to finding a buddy for your goal, you need someone who has your back, someone who will be honest with you and tell you straight when you're bullshitting yourself. This is the person you tell your secret goal to, rather than every person you meet. The more people you tell your intention to, the more diluted the energy required to execute it becomes, and you've talked yourself out of it.

CHAPTER 9

KICKING
NEGATIVE
HABITS

'Addiction begins in pain and ends in pain.'

– Eckhart Tolle

ADDICTION: SELF-MEDICATING

Canadian psychiatrist Dr Gabor Maté is famous for his pioneering work with addictive behaviour. For 12 years he worked in Downtown East Side, Vancouver, one of North America's most drug-afflicted areas. 'In my opinion,' he says, 'an addiction is manifested in any behaviour that a person finds temporary pleasure or relief in but suffers negative consequences as a result of and does not give up, or can't give up, despite those negative consequences.' The greater the suffering in our youth, adds Maté, the stronger the addiction in later life.

Addiction is a form of self-medication and provides escape from suffering and comfort from alienation. In other words, it's a pain reliever. The part of the brain that feels physical pain is also the same area that experiences emotional pain. Opiates, the choice of drug addicts, have been used in medicine for over 3,000 years. Marijuana, cocaine, opium (base heroin) and alcohol all possess not only mental but physical pain-relieving qualities. They work in the human brain because they resemble an internal opiate system operated by natural chemicals produced in our body called endorphins. Endorphins regulate the gut, the immune system and provide our brain with pain-relief. They also make possible the experiences of joy, pleasure and reward. The third function of endorphins is love, defined as the attraction which drives two bodies together with an attachment to take care of one another.

Dopamine, another vital chemical produced by the brain, is an incentive motivator, and is released in the *seeking* phase of hunger, or in the search for a sexual partner. It gives us feelings of happiness and euphoria, the feeling of being alive. Gambling, sex and shopping addictions all produce high dopamine levels.

Twenty-first-century science asserts the brain develops under the impact of its environment. In 2012 The Center on the Developing Child at Harvard University stated: 'The architecture of the brain is constructed by an ongoing process that begins before birth, continues into adulthood and establishes either a sturdy or fragile foundation for all the health learning and behaviour that follows.'

The most important ingredient in the formation of a healthy-minded adult is the quality of the parent–child relationship they experienced at a very young age. Consistent parenting, where the mother and father are responsive, happy, non-stressed, approachable and available in their care, produces the most balanced people. These conditions have to be present in the child's environment in order for their facets of self-regulation, stress regulation and emotional equilibrium to function normally as an adult. And if the right conditions aren't met? Brain scans of addicts have demonstrated that the impulse regulator, which controls our desires, is not working properly because something that happened in our environment when we were children stalled its development.

In the West, doctors ask, 'What's wrong with you?', when they should really be asking, 'What happened to you?' Instead of treating the symptoms, and separating the body from the mind, they should be looking at the cause. In other words, what happens to people emotionally affects their physiology. Adverse events experienced as kids can induce trauma (which comes from the ancient Greek word for wound) in later life, and left untreated, it will keep coming to the surface like a poisonous abscess. To understand our present dysfunction, it is our earlier self that we must return to.

UNDERSTANDING CHILDHOOD TRAUMA

My dad was a workhorse, fucking hell how he worked. We had a massive house with two fires, and my brother and I were constantly chopping wood to sustain them. This was between cleaning brass tables, taking the dogs out, and lowering down a Flymo lawnmower on a rope to cut the steep grass banks around the house; then cycling six miles to my grandad's house where we had to mow his orchards and his lawn ... jobs, jobs and more jobs. Friends even stopped calling in on me at home for fear they would be put to work. I thank my father for the discipline it instilled in me and the value of hard work, but really, it was just too much. As a kid you should have periods where you can just do your own thing. So, I rebelled against him, and when he left it was the best news in the world.

I can't remember much else about my childhood, the good times growing up with my brothers and sisters, it's clouded by too many memories of pain. The freakish trauma I experienced as a ten-year-old being attacked by a chimp is undoubtedly the Everest of my misadventures, but even before that I was impressively accident-prone. Every time we went on holiday my parents were nervous with anticipation that something bad would happen to me, because every year on holiday (with metronomic consistency) something *did* happen! I'd end up in some kind of bizarrely unlikely pickle, be it my shins being embedded with glass from the lemonade bottles I dropped in a French supermarket, to the hook episode when we holidayed in Lyme Regis and were line-fishing off the pier – I cast the line, and the hook, true to form, sunk itself deep into my leg. I might also mention that my chimp wounds turned gangrenous while on holiday, and I almost lost my arm.

The bottle, the chimp, the hook. It was almost like a pattern, a negative loop of accidents I seemed to be stuck in, or perhaps inviting? Even at home in Blighty, I was twice run over by cars, and twice in later life living in Australia. But back to the incident with the chimp; it seemed like it was the eye of the storm around whose gravitational pull other negative situations were attracted one after the other. BC (before chimp) I'd always been a little mischievous, that was just me, but AC (after chimp) I started getting into trouble with the police to the point they knew me by name. It was as if I'd inherited some of its feral genes.

William Wordsworth said 'the child is father to the man', and that observation is poignantly true, at least in my case, for as we've seen with the work of Dr Gabor Maté, as a kid you are an experience sponge. A massive percentage of your growth is based on those formative years up to the age of ten. It was also during this time I experienced the polar opposites of wealth and hardship. After my dad left, almost overnight we went from a wealthy family to a struggling family. From having everything we needed – nice clothes, cool toys, great Christmases – to having nothing. All around me, the household conversations went from abundance, which we had taken for granted, to lack. These sorry undertones of loss carried on into adulthood, for the issues I experienced with my finances – no matter how much I earned

I never had enough – hark back to the sudden *lack* I experienced as a child.

Violent trauma to the skin results in scar tissue growing over the wound. Unlike normal skin it is not flexible but rigid and masks feeling. Something similar happens with a deep trauma to the emotional self. Both lead to a hardening and loss of feeling. The essence of trauma is disconnection from the self, something I've experienced throughout my life as an addict, trying to heal a wound I couldn't see or touch with the aid of alcohol or drugs.

If you have the privilege of being a parent, it's so important to realise that the way you act around your kids, especially in their first ten years, will forge the later mindsets that govern how they live their lives. When I left my wife, I did so with good reason: we weren't right for each other and no matter what I might have tried, this harsh fact was never going to change. Square peg in a round hole. I was unhappy, restless and we brought out the worst in each other. It was clearly not the right environment in which to bring up my son, Luke. Many parents remain in this half-life for the benefit of their children but staying in such a comfort zone is detrimental to everybody involved. Pretending everything is okay when your kids can see right through the deceit creates issues for them later around commitment and love.

Maté believes if we are to be content as humans, we can no longer remain programmed by our childhood trauma, as prisoners of our past, dictated to by experience; we must make a conscious choice to live in the present. As long as you're aware of what happened to you and the impact it's had on you, you can begin to reprogram your response to it. It's about understanding yourself.

I'm 48 years of age as I write this book, and consider myself a happy person, but I'm lucky, in so far as I possess a brute determination and natural optimism that has outgrown much of my negative programming from those early years and my troubled teens, but to say that I'm healed completely of them would be a huge over-statement. I know I still have unfinished business with that near 40-year-old trauma of blood, flesh and teeth, and only one of us will win. But forgive me, I'm getting a little ahead of myself.

SOCIALISATION

We come into the world as creative, innocent human beings, born to imagine and produce amazing things. Sadly, this potential is short-lived, as we are swiftly socialised (or brainwashed) not only by the schooling system, but by our parents too. Each influences our thinking and behaviour away from our natural inclination towards joy to that of fear. We learn to moderate ourselves with *lack* rather than *abundance*, creating false ceilings for our ambitions, and limiting our right to be who we want to be.

Don't misunderstand me, both influences come from a place of good intention (usually). Maybe your parents raised you to worry about money, perhaps they grew up without much money themselves; maybe your parents pushed you towards a career rather than supported you in your decision to follow your passion. For people who grew up during the war, who came through the terror of nightly air raids, and lived during the post-war years of austerity and rationing, it's not surprising that they passed on their anxieties regarding money to their children, and through them their grandchildren with phrases like 'money doesn't grow on trees'.

Back in the Blitz, people were brought together by a common purpose to survive, to stick together, and during those harsh times found a sense of community. But I feel that we've lost that unity because everyone has become so competitive, so in their own silos, trying to 'keep up with the Joneses'. People won't talk genuinely to each other because they're scared of showing any sign of weakness or lack of wealth. They're buying things they can't afford, and it's all about the image. People are living enslaved in that. Their only goal in life is to look like they're doing well regardless of whether they are or not. In fact, they happily sacrifice their feelings over the visual and material representation.

I was very much the same as everyone else. We go through life and buy what we're supposed to, we follow as told. We're not shepherds, we're sheep. We're told: 'You must have achieved this by the time you're 25'; 'You must have a mortgage and a settled job to be socially respectable'; 'You must have kids'. And for most they get to a point where they can then simply plateau, looking to the left and right and say, 'Yep this will do, this is now safe,' and commence their maintenance programme to sustain the lifestyle they have created, losing any enthusiasm to improve and grow beyond that point. Meanwhile, their health and happiness declines!

I think these prescriptive destinies we're allotted are a trap to keep us locked in the system, in society. I too fell into that. I got married, bought a house, had a child. I lived in a Barrett home on an estate, and the only distinction between the identical houses, was the size and make of the cars parked outside. It was mundane, monotone and utterly limiting. I was working in a job as a soldier that paid me barely anything. Ultimately, that's why I left the Forces, that's why a lot of us left. But I didn't help my situation with the amount of financial pressure I put on myself. I never seemed to have enough money. And as I've said, it stems back to my childhood, that severe lack, and my obsessive fear of not having enough.

We and we alone have the power to renounce the patterns of socialised 'herd' thinking and to start drawing on the wisdom of our inner self which has no boundaries to what it can do.

CHAPTER 10

DEMON DAYS

THE BANSHEE CALLS

My brother and I had been living in separate countries for 18 years by the time I decided to return to England to set up Break-Point. Excited at the prospect of seeing my family, I phoned my brother from Australia. 'Mate, I'm coming home for good.'

'That's amazing!' he said. 'I'm so happy to hear it. However, I'm leaving.'

'What?'

'Yeah, I've got a job in Malaysia, and I leave just after you arrive.'

Of course, I was gutted, but the silver lining here was that because of him leaving, my mum was moving from her house in Cornwall to look after his home, which left her cottage empty. Returning with empty pockets, a house to stay in pretty much rent-free was a massive help. Here, I could finally get myself focused on Break-Point, and for a limited amount of time would not be ghosted by the need to keep working constantly. Unbeknown to me, the Universe was laying the foundations for me before I even knew what I was going to do.

Mum's place was a cute little house in Hayle, my outgoings were minimal, and I was doing the odd bit of work here and there to keep afloat. I began to plan my own personal bootcamp in 2014, and top of the priority list was getting my drinking under control.

Deep down, if I'm honest, I didn't think for a moment I could ever *really* totally stop. My relationship with booze was like an illicit affair with a beautiful but dangerous woman that leaves you bleeding but still enraptured, and despite the fact you know she's a banshee and will suck the life from you then move onto her next victim, you keep leaving the back door open for her. I was fighting the constant tension of not having booze in the house but wanting it terribly, dreaming of chasing the weekend again and kicking back with *her* on the sofa. When I went cold turkey, the banshee sent the demons chattering around my bed in the dark, a night of cold sweats, ghosts and insomnia. In order to delay the latter, those one-day sessions would turn into three-day binges, followed by another three days' recovery; I was losing so much time.

HUMP DAY

'Hump day'. I hate the word. What's hump day? It's Wednesday. People call it this because once you get over the midweek hump you're well on your way to the weekend. So many are living their lives for Friday – Monday, Tuesday, Wednesday and Thursday are redundant, just blocks of time to get through till fantastic Friday.

If you only live for the weekend, something is missing, and you deserve more. Every day for me is a blessing. To me it's not Wednesday or Thursday, it's another day full of opportunity. But when I first got to Cornwall and was preparing for the bootcamp, I too was a hump-day believer. And by way of reward for reaching the weekend, I put poison into my body, polluting all the good work I'd done. It was as if I was a child and needed a present.

Time kills even more dreams than doubt. It paves the way for the justification of failure. As humans we're shortcut-focused and will do anything to reduce the amount of time and effort it takes to do something, not bother doing it properly and fail quickly or simply not even try at all. Admittedly, we all need to live with time because everything in the modern world is based around the clock, but we should be conscious of it rather than being its slave. The more you can remove yourself from it the better. You might think most of life's surprises are over and one day is the same as the next but this isn't so. You can find new things all the time, you just have to design your life in such a way that there is sufficient time to notice them. Most of us are moving too quickly to realise this. When you're passive to time, when you're not in control of alcohol, relationships, finances, health, you are living by the clock. Instead, you need to be the commander of all those things, as if any one of them has the upper hand with you, you become their gimp.

I knew that if I was to become Battle Ready and actualise my dream of creating my company, then I needed to get 'dry' first. I didn't say to myself, 'I'm going to give up for life,' but like the 12 Steps programme followed by members of Alcoholics Anonymous, I would conduct my abstinence on a day-by-day basis. I said to myself, 'I'm going to give up drinking for eight weeks.' It seemed a bearable, achievable period of time.

The simple reason for my wanting to give up was it was affecting my clarity of judgement, productivity and creativity. I knew I'd achieve so much more when my mind wasn't diluted with alcohol. I'd experienced periods of such intense clarity that I understood how powerful the mind could be, and its need for positive intent and visualisation to help it flourish. If I clouded this, I wasn't going to deliver the dreams I was focused on achieving, for even in its lowest form, booze was affecting my mental stability and focus. I was also so very conscious how negative booze made me feel in the long term. It was typically 'Short-term comfort for long-term pain', which was the opposite of what I was looking for.

I recently came across this information:

Alcohol is said to have come from the Arabic term, 'Al-Khul' and 'Al-Gawl' which means 'Body Eating Spirit'. Perhaps this is why alcoholic drinks are called 'spirits'. Drinking alcohol is one of the fastest things you can do to lower your vibration, as it's been used as a tool to keep human consciousness at a lowered state for thousands of years.

My thoughts totally align with this as I feel alcohol has suppressed my productivity and creativity for much of my adult life.

In the first days of the bootcamp I'd say to myself, 'What am I going to do on a Friday, when all my mates are calling?' I felt deprived of something. But then I'd progress to realising that the only thing I was depriving myself of was time, and how many precious hours I had already lost. As I started to recover from my dependence, I began to fill the gaps with positive and productive things and before I knew it, I was looking back, thinking, 'How did I ever have time to drink?' I heard that beautiful banshee calling to me from the mire of my 3 a.m. dreams, gasping for a drink, but I didn't let her in. Mostly.

When you stop living in the future when you imagine life will be perfect, and instead start appreciating what you've got in the present, your life becomes fuller and more balanced. Newfound sobriety is like a fog that lifts around you so you can see things clearly in the sunlight once again. Some people will say, 'You must have such a boring life, now you don't drink any more,' but it's the opposite. You lead a more interesting life because it's more present, full of surprises and less predictable than if you're just drinking to mark time. I experience moments more deeply, and value every day now. Someone recently stated, 'You're only here once!' 'Exactly!' I replied.

WHAT'S THE PURPOSE?

In those precious three months that were to form the bootcamp that ultimately saved my life, I finally started questioning the long-term benefits of my affair with alcohol. 'What is the purpose of you drinking?' I asked myself. Alcohol was such a massive part of my life at the time, but when I questioned its actual purpose and couldn't list any successes I'd had while on the sauce, it became obvious that for me it was a waste of time and it made me hate myself. There was nothing, absolutely nothing to recommend it, so why have it in my life? I used the purpose pyramid and couldn't tick one value!

If you're doing something that's only offering you short-term euphoria but no long-term gain, you need to question its worth. We need to hold to account the purpose of everything in our lives that might be holding us back. I'm not saying that's the same for everyone; some of you may like a regular tipple but that's all it is, you know when to stop. But when something's got control of you and is steering you rather than the other way around, you need to deal with it. Money had control of me, alcohol had control of me, just as a co-dependent relationship had once had possession of me until I moved to that flat on my own in Brisbane and began to relish my own company.

So many times before I'd felt the numbness course through me as I touched my lips to a drink, and I never questioned it: I was drink's bitch, chained by my neck to her ankle. But gradually, the more I questioned the purpose of taking a drink, the easier it became to be able to recognise a break point; it was only a second but that was all I needed to be able to process the harm it would cause and start to resist, to fight back.

My choice was either continued addiction, dismantling my life for short-term comfort and long-term discomfort; or taking a break point and going through short-term discomfort for the long-term gain. When you don't have a goal and therefore a focus, you leave the door wide open for all the negative things in your life to wander in. But I had a very clear purpose and it meant a great deal to me.

ONE-METRE SQUARE

When you're in the white heat of the battle with addiction you must forget about the bigger picture. Bring it back to one-metre square: just focus on everything that's right in front of you. This will help get you through this moment and avoid any negative externals that could infect your thinking. It's a case of looking out for the break points in your immediate vicinity. With a little practice, they start to appear like cat's eyes glowing in the darkness and a road opens up for you to follow, so long as you focus on what's right in front of you. I was climbing Mt Blanc recently, and when I first took in the enormity of Europe's tallest mountain, I thought, 'How the fuck am I going to get up there?' But instead of looking up I focused on my feet moving step by step. When I finally did look up again, the summit was so much closer. I glanced back to see how far I'd come, admired the stunning view and kept climbing. It's not all about reaching the top, but savouring the journey to reach it, enjoying each moment, and occasionally looking back on your achievement so far to spur you on. It's easy to get fixated on where you want to be, but time should be taken to raise your head, look back and give yourself a pat on the back because nine times out of ten no one else will be there to do so.

It's the same when dealing with addiction. Don't look too far in front of you, keep going one foot in front of the other, and before you know it, you've lasted the day, then two days, then a week and then a month. You'll be able to look back and see how far you've come. You'll feel good about the progress you've made. You still don't need to look directly at the summit, but perhaps you can afford a peek. It won't be so daunting now.

Alcohol can provide short-term euphoria. I used to have a drink and become creative. It might help me have ideas, but when it came to long-term achievement, or implementing those ideas, I was too scared to do anything. I was living in a state of fear. I might try to convince myself that alcohol was great for that creative mindset, but it wasn't. When it came to action, I would never follow through.

I feel a lot of people have self-medicated and become addicted because of a vacuum of purpose in themselves. When we experience that void – through any kind of addiction – it's not because we're losers, it's because we've got nothing in our life that's channelling our energy, which leads to low self-worth. For me it was silencing the mind-chatter, that nauseating voice. The booze successfully numbed it, closed it down. It also helped me deal with my existential boredom. Sobriety seemed a monochrome, sterile place. Now and again, like Withnail threatening to install a jukebox in the Penrith Tea Rooms, I needed to change the dynamic with a few fireworks and paint the weekend red.

Your mind will push you to chase something. And if you don't focus it on the things that benefit your life, it'll choose for you. It has a choice of 70,000–100,000 daily thoughts to feed on, and it will engage with something in there, so it's about you being the dictator and orchestrator of your thoughts, not their victim. The human mind doesn't know the difference between a good habit and a bad habit. It doesn't know the difference between good and evil. It just makes sure that we're engaged and focused on something. And that's why it's so important for everyone to have conscious focus and direction of their energy.

If you're passive to those 70,000–100,000 thoughts that rush through your mind every day, you're unaware of what you're growing in your Thought Farm, and given our default setting, your thoughts will most likely be heading somewhere negative. Even positive people are prone to negative thoughts; it's not protocol for us to think positively. The caveman didn't walk out of his cave looking for a unicorn, instead he came out thinking, 'Holy shit, what's going to kill me today!?'

That's just the way we're geared, and while it makes sense (so far as survival of the species is concerned) to look at any situation and consider what might go wrong, it should not be allowed to block our right to joy and abundance.

THE DEVIL'S TRIDENT

Addiction, like the Devil's trident, has three prongs: fear, lack of purpose and trauma. You may have been scarred by something when you were younger, but you've managed to keep a lid on it most of the time; you occasionally go off the rails for a bit but then get back on track. You may well be blocking out your trauma, blanketing it in addiction. In Baghdad, when I was working on the job my head was consumed with business stuff, but I used to hit the drink every time I came away from there because the trauma was going on in my head. And the simple solution was drink or substance abuse, or whatever. I thought that self-medicating was my only route, or maybe I didn't think at all, reaching for the substance that was going to numb me most, when in fact what I needed was to accept what had happened to me and move forward.

Life is tough. People will let you down, walk all over you, cheat on you, and people close to you will die. You need to understand that there's going to be hardships in life and it's not going to be a smooth ride. I also think it's a lot harder these days with the addition of social media, because you've got all these dream lifestyles presented to you every time you turn on your phone or computer, all of which is bullshit and about as authentic as a second-hand-car-dealer's promise. And because our lives don't match up to the fake dream, and because we are not prepared for life's curveballs, bereavement and betrayal, it hits us hard in the gut and leaves us reeling and out of breath. *Resilio* is the old Greek word for the ability to spring back into the same shape, and modern-day society is just not resilient any more. The bottom line is that being popular on social media is like being rich in Monopoly.

There's a big difference between believing you have a right to be happy and live your life the way you want to, and somebody who is stuck with a sense of entitlement who thinks, 'It should come to me. I'm owed this.' You must generate abundance yourself; you shouldn't wait for it to come to you. And when you are in vibration, in tune with the natural flow of the Universe, life is so much easier; there are fewer major ups-and-downs, less drama, just a natural, contented flow. Once you begin to trust the flow and your inner wisdom, it's amazing how resilient you become. You realise the Universe hasn't got it in for you and you're an integral component of life's fabric. Everything is connected: when we die, we're recycled into the soil, our genetic make-up *is* the Universe. We need to learn not to get overly emotionally attached to success, nor to trauma. It's about keeping an even balance of your emotional state, living in the now and maintaining the flow in yourself.

I'm grateful for where I am, but I put in the hard work to get to this point. I cleared the skeletons out of my closet, hosed away the addictions, and learned to remove the negativity from my thinking as soon as I heard it carping in my head. And only because of these measures have I been able to access the inner me, the flow that has started giving me exactly what I want in life. We need to declutter, realise that it doesn't serve us to hang on to trauma, what's the point? Don't let it define you – stick it in the fucking bin!

The more you live within your limits, the less fulfilling your life. It all comes back to spotting your break points, having goals, and pushing into the discomfort of the short term for the long-term gain. The military and the Special Forces gave me a good foundation to take my next step in life, but I believe I've achieved and learned so much more outside of the military. The military never made me, it just prepared me for what was ahead.

Everyone has break points throughout the day. Everyone. I know when that Shortcut Syndrome is operating, when I don't want to dot the Is and cross the Ts, and that makes me want to fight it even more, because it's my default negativity system creating self-doubt to prevent the goal from happening. We're all fallible and it's a constant battle. Just this morning I was sitting in bed thinking, 'I should go out for a run. I should definitely go out for a run …' Only, I spent too long thinking so I never went. If you begin to think about doing something, the mind will always say, 'Well, tomorrow you're up early and then you're going to be working late for the next three weeks, so you deserve a break, have a lie-in.' Sometimes we do need to rest and listen to our body and be kind to it: 'You're tired, time to go to bed', or 'Don't take that run today because you're absolutely knackered', but most of the time your mind is looking for an excuse not to go.

I decided to give alcohol another go and after a little peer pressure from the lads from *SAS: Who Dares Wins* I got back on it while filming series four in Chile in October 2018 after two and a half years without a drop. I thought that maybe I was missing out and now that I was the master of control it was something I could pick up and put down when I felt like it. I drank for nine months which were, looking back, nine months of bad choices; skipping training days and eating food that simply wasn't akin to a healthy lifestyle.

The last time I touched a drop was during a recce to the Isle of Skye for series five of *SAS: Who Dares Wins*. I drank every night that week and on my return home to Shropshire, late on a Friday night, my girlfriend was away for the weekend and I had the house all to myself. Just me and my black lab, Murphy. I'd had a few drinks with Billy (Mark Billingham, my fellow DS on the show) at the airport earlier that day and in the taxi on the way home. The next morning, I woke and got up quite late, and already that mindset of: 'You've had a hard week...' had established itself, and I just sat in my lounge, vacant as a zombie. It was nice weather outside, a beautiful blue autumn day, but instead of getting out in it, I put a film on. And as the film started I was just sitting there when I said to myself, 'What the fuck are you doing?' but then my mind counter-punched with, 'You've had a hard week, Ollie. You deserve this lazy time.' Then the 'What's the purpose?' question, which has now become a habit, sprung up in my head. 'If you hadn't been drinking would you still be doing this, sitting inside on a glorious day? No, you'd be in the gym, you'd be up the hills with Murphy.' And it was at that point I told myself, 'I'm not drinking again.' That was the last time I had a drink. Sometimes you have to revisit the past to reconfirm why you gave it up in the first place. Like a random meeting with an ex shortly after your break-up, which rarely ends well.

Regardless of whether you're a lawyer, surfer, an astronaut, or working in a laundrette, cutting out or cutting right down the amount you drink will improve your life. It was vital that I re-evaluated what I was doing and compared what I would have been doing if I wasn't drinking. Unless I'd had the last few years' experience of how much more productivity I get out of my days when sober, it would have been easy for me to have gone down to the pub, had a couple of pints, and slide back into that cycle again.

PART III

HOW TO CHANGE

CHAPTER 11

BOOTCAMP

In 1971, Muhammad Ali established 'Fighter's Heaven', his new training camp in rural Pennsylvania, at a place called Deer Lake. Here he trained for his most famous fights, 'Rumble in the Jungle' ('74) and 'Thrilla in Manilla' ('75). At the side of the road that snaked up the mountain past his cabin, he placed boulders upon which Ali painted the names of his greatest adversaries: Sonny Liston, George Foreman, Joe Frasier ... As he ran up this road clocking thousands of miles of roadwork, the names of those leviathans would remind him of his past triumphs and inspire him for his next challenge. Mum's cottage was my Deer Lake, and upon my imaginary boulders were the names of my greatest foes: Jack, Jim and Johnnie; the difference being, I was yet to beat them.

Fresh from Australia I started my own bootcamp, one that incorporated process, habit-building routine, positive affirmations, meditation, nutrition and exercise. I made sure I didn't read any newspapers or watch TV, all of it was inflammatory unnecessary mental noise. Nor did I allow myself to go near my phone. Newspapers veer towards the alarmist and the negative to sell more copies, while TV news is no different. If you're not careful it's easy to start thinking that there's no good left in the world and the apocalypse is imminent. I think the more fear the system disseminates, the more malleable and passive the population becomes. We wouldn't consciously put fuel in our cars which would strip the engine and affect its smooth running, and yet we insist on filling our mind with yet more worry by swallowing the crap thrown at us by the media daily.

First, I had to be extremely honest with who and where I was in life. It's easy to spend your life comparing yourself with others, that's what we do as humans. Comparing with people more fortunate than you enforces need and stems from jealousy. You say to yourself that you wish you were them or you want to be just like them. This is toxic and the vibration you emit is so far from what you're comparing with. It's time to level with yourself and appreciate exactly where you are. From here you have a foundation that's relative to you and no one else. This is the foundation that will establish a root structure big enough to sustain the imminent growth, as opposed to a tree that falls over once the wind hits it.

I resolutely policed the input going into my mind and avoided anything negative. In order to change things in my life I knew I needed to take a good look at myself and create an infrastructure, a process that I could adhere to to move things forward. The change had to come from me internally before anything would change externally, and that call had happened when I left Sarah. But it had taken this long for me to find my purpose and now I had to break down my goals as well break the back of my alcohol addiction. I started off every day with meditation and self-affirmations and then I exercised. As well as reading self-development books, I cut out all processed foods in favour of wholesome, healthy organics. I bought a clean A4 notepad and started drawing up everything I wanted to achieve as well as listening to podcasts framed around personal development and positivity, and Ted Talks. I cleansed myself internally by being conscious of what I was eating from the moment I woke to the moment I went to bed. Dairy and red meat were eliminated, and I increased my intake of green vegetables.

I consumed only distilled water and if I felt a little crazy, I would add some ice and lemon! My Cornish bootcamp established this regime and it was to last two months. Every day I had to battle constant doubt, an imaginary audience of a thousand critics following me around everywhere, mocking me and my grand goal. I had an internal battle of good and bad and it was time to enter the ring and step toe-to-toe.

At first, trying to build a better version of myself was hard as there were so many deeply buried voices from my past saying, 'What a waste of time. This isn't working ...' added to which I didn't particularly like who I was. 'I am ready to accept change, as difficult as it may seem, I know I am being prepared for bigger and better things.'

I found an official contract template and made it out to myself, stating a date and an intention – a contract with myself – and read it out loud to my reflection in the mirror every morning. At first, I felt like a dick as my imaginary audience laughed and joked at me, but the more I repeated it the more that it began to feel more natural and familiar; besides, if you can't look yourself in the eye and tell yourself what you want, how can you ever expect to achieve it? After a few days I started to gain confidence in my belief (I even believed it), and I told myself exactly what I was going to achieve. All the while I kept reassuring myself, 'This visualisation stuff works, it *works* ... you nearly died because of it in Iraq when you summoned that attack so you could extend your contract with ABC News ... you brought it to you by visualising it. Remember that.'

But after the first few weeks nothing had happened, apart from my feeling fitter and healthier, and it was getting to a point where I needed something from the Universe, proof of all my efforts. I started saying, 'Give me something, however small, to show that

I'm not going mad. Show me a sign that I'm on the right track …'
Eventually I did get a sign and it was by no means 'small'. The
problem was I was coming from a place of lack: 'I need this, I
need (want) that.' When I look back now, the Universe had something a lot bigger to show me, because the amount of effort I put
into clearly envisaging my future company Break-Point was literally every minute of every day: pure focus, and the theory behind
Break-Point was exactly the process I was engaged in. So, when I
look at it that way, something life-changing was building, entirely
relative to the amount I was focusing on it, and naturally that
took more time to reveal itself.

Part of that focus was about keeping my mindset pure and
being brutal with negative influences. As best I could, I removed
every possible source of influence that might dampen my equilibrium and drive. I surrounded myself with positive mantras. It was
a very disciplined and regimented atmosphere. As well as reading
positive thinking books, the most influential and thought provoking
of which was Eckhart Tolle's *A New Earth*, I also tried acupuncture
to help stop drinking. The more I focused on its lack of purpose and
the things I wanted to achieve; the less powerful alcohol became. A
lot of people would say that drinking is an integral part of their job
because they go out networking, meet other people, and that alcohol
is a good enabler for conversation. My response to this is it depends
on the individual; if you have a dependency on drinking and it is
controlling you, then it's not a positive at all. On top of that people
are more addicted to alcohol then they are the networking so all in
all what they are doing is simply notworking. For me, personally,
there was no purpose or value in drinking. I knew the departure of
it was the answer to unlocking my potential.

Asking ourselves on a constant basis, 'What's the purpose of
this, how is it benefiting me?' is a very powerful self-assessment

tool, and a brutal exposer of that which is bad for us. As soon as we start addressing ourselves without bullshit, targeting the efficacy of external things in our lives, huge changes start happening. You'll start questioning your jobs, your personal relationships, your need to buy expensive cars or be seen in certain restaurants. The rewards of investing in yourself and your inner life come thick and fast.

I have to mention here that the purpose for this is to change the blueprint. Forty-three years of programming simply can't be changed by acknowledging you don't like something about your life. We have to build new neurons and make them super-highways of new positive habits.

MAKING A CONTRACT WITH YOURSELF

A self-contract that you design and read to yourself every morning is a great way to keep focused on your goal. You should stick to one overarching goal and set a deadline for the contract. Keep the wording of the agreement simple and clear, stating what you want to achieve, how you'll achieve it and how it will positively impact your life. Don't place your focus on the penalties of not following through with it, but rather the positive outcomes. Nobody likes to break a promise, and by signing it and saying it to your reflection repeatedly in the mirror each morning, you're making an agreement with yourself which you won't want to break. If you're unsure of whether you'll stick to your self-contract, enlist a trusted friend, mentor or respected colleague to co-sign a hard copy as a witness. But pick this person carefully, for close friends and families often give us well-meant advice that attempts to dissuade us from attempting what seem to them unrealistic or overly challenging goals.

EXERCISE: MAKE YOUR OWN CONTRACT

Here's an example to guide you:

I (your name) _____

on this day, (insert date) _____

hereby state my intention of achieving (insert goal),

_____

by (insert date) _____

and give my personal promise to follow the programme I
have designed for myself (insert details on the process/steps
to achieving your goal)_____

_____.

For the duration of the programme I will remain focused
and disciplined, implementing and executing all my designs
to the best of my ability.

The area of my life that I will impact during my personal
bootcamp will be (insert here – it could be health, finances,
whatever it is you want to change)_____

_____.

Signed

Witness

MORNING ROUTINE

The way you start the day is integral to what you achieve in it and how it ends. My morning routine means that I take myself to the day and dominate over it. If your life is governed by the resentment of waking, followed by repetitive snooze button interrogation, you're heading to the dark side of every day.

It should look something a little like this:

- Wake
- Positive affirmation
- Make your bed
- Do not take your phone off flight mode
- Avoid looking at your phone. Avoid all emails. Be selfish. This is your time.
- Read your personal contract out loud to yourself while looking in a mirror. Do it somewhere quiet without distractions. If you want to put your stamp on the day, the earlier in the morning, the better.
- Meditation – while you are reading the contract start to visualise in your mind's eye what the goal you have chosen not only looks like but also feels like. Paint the picture, use all your senses. Allow yourself to live the moment as if it's already happened.
- Lemon and hot water – no coffee or tea
- Exercise
- Eat
- Battle Ready for the day

This is exactly how I started, and it changed my life. It was difficult to do but the only way you can change your habits is to engage in a process that is void of emotions, feelings and judgement. The only question is: How much do you want to change?

Remember: 'Persistence kills resistance'.

Over time my routine hasn't differed too much and now looks like this:

0500 – Wake & Rise like a Polaris missile!

0515 – Power cocktail:

   Organic and dried powder:

   1 tbsp grated lemon peel

   ½ tsp cinnamon

   1 tsp turmeric

   ½ tsp ginger

   ½ tsp cayenne pepper

   1 tsp Celtic salt

   1 tbsp apple cider vinegar

   1 tbsp MCT oil

Method – Place ingredients in a cup of hot water and mix with milk frother, add dash of cold water to cool and drink with straw so you don't look like a hardened smoker from the turmeric.

Reason – When you sleep your body goes into a period of forced starvation (fasting), it's ready and waiting to absorb whatever is given to it. Although I'm not averse to a coffee, caffeine is a toxin and the energy you feel from this is your body reacting to the poison. The ingredients above are super foods and all play an amazing part in your health.

0530 – Guided meditation. This is my focused attention at my intention, for the day, the week and for my specific goal.

0600 – Run or gym.

0700 – Answer or send emails to keep opportunities in momentum. This is when I turn on my phone and check social media. Rest of UK starts to get up.

0800 – Ready to dominate.

POSITIVE AFFIRMATIONS

In Australia, 2014, I knew change was upon me. I'd started getting more in tune with my thoughts and the beginnings of my newly found spiritual education, empowered by a daily positive affirmation: 'I am willing to accept change, as difficult as it may seem. I know I am destined for bigger and better things.'

At the time I had said this repeatedly with no idea or knowledge of where I wanted to be or what I was going to do. My contract with the oil company was coming to an end and change was looming, which scared me as I'd got so used to the comfort of a steady wage and a nice apartment overlooking the Brisbane River. I didn't have a plan and then one morning, I woke at 3 a.m. and, summoned to attention with a thought that contradicted my very being, I was suddenly wide awake and being directed to the thought of moving back to the UK, almost like a secret code had opened a door to a forbidden area. I decided to allow the thought to gather some momentum. It was something that I had fought against for so long, but perhaps this was my calling to return?

And as I said earlier, within two weeks I had sold everything and was on a plane 'destined for bigger and better things', but all I had to go on was a vison, an insight; I was still very much in the midst of short-term discomfort.

What are 'positive affirmations' or 'self-affirmations'? In simple terms, they are positive sentences – always set in the present tense – that you repeat to yourself again and again with the sole intention of making the mantra real. Remember, your brain doesn't know the difference between reality and what you tell it, so by saying you're feeling positive even if this is not the case will send this message to your brain which then transmits the feeling to the rest of your body, and before you know it you *do* feel better.

When you first start using affirmations such as: 'I am healthy, financially stable and in control of my life', it might not be true. But over time the consistent repetition of this daily, positive affirmation will reshape your belief about yourself, giving you a more positive perception of who you are, while the finances, health and self-control take shape in tandem. After a couple of weeks, you'll be your own best believer.

Given that your brain is a creature of habit and strengthens connections every time you repeat an action or a thought until it becomes second nature, by seeding the same message to it again and again, it quickly adopts this as true and makes it happen. A quote I love is from a guy called Bob Proctor: 'If you can hold it in your head, you can hold it in your hands.' It's so true. Affirmations are especially useful in times of fear, weakness, self-doubt and when making big chances to your life. Self-esteem and confidence can be increased through affirmations, as can the appetite for exercise, losing weight, in fact pretty much anything you put your mind to. The more tension there is between the current reality and the goal the better, for the brain always seeks to fix discomfort. In other words, if you have an affirmation that seems a long way from your current experience to the extent that it feels awkward repeating it – maybe it's something like: 'I am wealthy and have a good relationship with money' – your brain will help you make changes to your lifestyle to make it come true. Remember Bruce Lee telling himself he was not only going to walk again but be the first Pan-Asian action superstar? We are what we tell ourselves and some of us are naturally better at it than others, but we all have the capacity for imagination within us.

Everybody said the four-minute mile couldn't be broken until Roger Bannister finally smashed it. On the morning of his run on 24 July 1954, he wasn't focusing on the fact he had never achieved this in the past, nor that he never would in the future; instead he was in flow with himself in the present. And as you probably know, it wasn't just his own personal best he broke that day as well as setting a new world record, he also broke down that negative spectre holding all distance runners back; namely that it was impossible to run a sub-four-minute mile. Interesting that within a few months of his achievement several athletes would go on to do the same. Why? Because they gave themselves permission to imagine doing the same as Bannister, knowing that it was now achievable, even though it had been achievable all along. They simply unlocked potential that was withheld due to the limitation they had personally framed around it.

Think about it a moment. What is it that you are visualising – creating a global brand, losing five stone, running your first 5K race on a prosthetic limb, walking across the Gobi Desert to raise funds for cancer research? The chances are these admirable feats have been done before and you are just as capable as those individuals who have already gone where you wish to go, so take heart from their achievement, give yourself permission to succeed knowing that it is entirely possible and within your grasp.

The power of affirmations lies in their ability to transform your external world by first changing your internal one. As new, more positive beliefs form in your mind, it becomes progressively easier to create what you want in life, no matter what it is. Daily affirmations help you vibrate in alignment with abundance rather than lack, enabling you to manifest your goals more quickly. They also make you more aware of your thought processes, allowing you to recognise and challenge negative thoughts as they arise. Positive affirmations enhance personal happiness as well as providing a much-needed shot of self-belief.

MORNING AFFIRMATION

When we go into sleep mode our lizard brain, or inner chimp as it's often referred to, sits on guard, hardwired to protect us. As we know he's been doing it for hundreds of thousands of years. When you wake up in the morning the chimp is finishing up his nightly vigil and he's tired and cranky, and if you're not careful he can ruin the start of your day with negative expectations; see how quickly, and we're talking seconds here, your thoughts turn to worry in the morning when you stir awake.

So, morning affirmations are about starting with a positive outlook rather than a passive one. I go to meet the day, the day does not come to me. And to do this, to put my mark on it and access a positive mood that will radiate through the day, I have a very structured process to keep me in check. Early rise around 5am, followed by meditation and morning affirmations. Your morning needs to begin with a positive affirmation before the ego has a chance to start looking for negatives. As soon as you wake up in the morning a mantra as simple as, 'Today's going to be an amazing day full of opportunities,' can get you off to a good start. Remember, your brain will do what it's told to, so even if it's pissing down outside and you feel flat as a pancake, tell your brain otherwise. Here's some examples you can use if you're struggling to think of a mantra.

- Today I'm looking forward to having a great productive day.
- Difficult as it seems, every day I am one step closer to my goals.
- I feel grateful for the opportunities that will come my way today.
- Today I am going to be kind to myself and do as much as I can.
- I am not scared of failure, I embrace change and welcome abundance.
- I accept blessings and abundance into my life.
- I am healthy, happy and determined.

EXERCISE: POSITIVE AFFIRMATIONS AND MORNING AFFIRMATIONS

Affirmations are proven methods of self-improvement because of their ability to rewire our brains. Much like exercise, they raise the level of feel-good hormones and push our brains to form new clusters of 'positive thought' neurons. In the sequence of thought-speech-action, affirmations play an integral role by breaking patterns of negative thoughts, negative speech, and, in turn, negative actions.

Examples of Positive Affirmations:

- I am superior to negative thoughts and low actions.
- I possess the qualities needed to be extremely successful.
- My ability to conquer my challenges is limitless; my potential to succeed is infinite.

How to Create Positive Affirmations
1. Start with the words 'I am...'
2. Use the present tense.
3. State it in the positive.
4. Keep it brief.
5. Make it specific.
6. Include an action word ending with –ing.
7. Include at least one dynamic emotion or feeling word.
8. Make affirmations for yourself, not others.

Spend time coming up with an affirmation that supports your goal. Practise saying your positive affirmation as soon as you wake and the negativity starts to flow or at any time you are feeling negative about your positive actions.

Write down three positive sentences, in the present tense, about how you would like to be. Don't be afraid to set the bar high. Then repeat these sentences first thing in the morning and when you get up.

1. _____

_____

_____

_____

_____

2. _____

_____

_____

_____

_____

3. _____

_____

_____

_____

_____

AVOID SOCIAL NETWORKING
FIRST THING IN THE MORNING

I often fantasise about coming off the grid and having one of the old burner (phone-only) mobiles, with no internet on it. For many of us, the first thing we do on waking is reach for our mobile phone to check our emails, news feeds or social-network sites. Aside from wasting valuable time, your positive mood can be instantly swayed towards the negative by reading a disappointing email or a misguided comment on your social feed. As soon as you turn on your mobile device you lose your connection with yourself, while social networking makes you vulnerable – almost co-dependent – on the volume of your *likes*, on that very reward system.

It's a problem that so many people's self-esteem is based on how many followers they've got on Instagram, the likes they receive, or even better, encouraging comments for their photographic dispatches and disclosures of their lives. There are still a few wild places on Earth where the indigenous people refuse to be photographed because they believe they are giving up part of their soul. I wonder if they know just how right they are? For even though these people are living in the technological equivalent of the Middle Ages with no phones or electricity and an inability to project themselves and their perfect house / meal / lifestyle / girlfriend / smile across continents in seconds, what they do have is authenticity and self-governance. They haven't handed over the right to others – be it strangers or friends – to determine with a thumbs-up emoji whether or not they feel wanted or irrelevant.

We need to redefine how often we use these things. First of all, there was Friends Reunited, not awfully user-friendly or sexy to look at but handy if you wanted to track down an old mate or former flame. The next incarnation (by a completely different creator) was much stealthier and more appealing. It was called Facebook and though it offered the same function as Friends Reunited of tracking down long-lost people with the press of a button, it also enabled them to be a part of your day via posting what they were up to with photographs and videos, presenting an altogether more intimate window into their lives. And you could be flirty too with a 'poke', you could 'love' and 'like'. These windows allowed you to comment on whether or not you liked their new purchase or celebrate with them that they felt happy or blessed … And in return they would hopefully do the same for you, and each time a harmless little poke licked your ear and warmed your cockles you experienced a little reward, a frisson of something you grew to love.

Before you knew it you looked forward to getting messages from these new friends (or old friends, or people who had never been your friends at school) who were generous enough to trawl you and every other creature they'd ever met, in their long-line gill nets as they dragged along with their global circle of friends. And as we became blissfully lost in the glow of our cyber honeymoon, we never knew that algorithms more intelligent than their Facebook creators had been developed to track and assess our browsing patterns, comments and dislikes. No wonder Facebook was worth hundreds of millions in no time at all. They held the ultimate key to power: knowledge; for while we were happily oblivious to what was happening to us, Facebook had a pretty good idea of the monster they were creating. Validation from others was the drug we craved and took in multiple shots, and in our glazed stupefaction up popped those ads of holidays we'd dreamed of or clothes we'd expressed an interest in, targeted with sniper precision.

Without our knowing but entirely within the founders' intent, we became a victim of a social-modification empire, of which there are now a number, including Facebook, Twitter, Pinterest, Google and Instagram, all of them valuable data banks and fertile predatory ground for advertisers. When we begin to realise that our ego is the one that allowed us to get washed along and taken in by all this crap, we can begin to see these social networks for what they are, and for what we are to them: little lab rats in a vast cyber-maze experiencing dopamine hits of pleasure each time we receive a like or a nice comment.

As Jaron Lanier, the Silicon Valley scientist renowned for spilling the beans on the dangers of social media, asserts in his brilliant book *Ten Arguments for Deleting Your Social Networks Right Now*:

> *When people get a flattering response in exchange for posting something on social media, they get in the habit of posting more. That sounds innocent enough, but it can be the first stage of an addiction that becomes a problem for individuals and society ... When many people are addicted to manipulative schemes the world gets dark and crazy.*

Sean Parker, ex-first president of Facebook, now admits, 'It's a social validation feedback loop ... exploiting a vulnerability in human psychology ... it changes your relationship with society, with each other. God only knows what it's doing to our children's brains.' And former vice-president of user growth at Facebook, Chamath Palihapitiya, adds:

> *The short-term dopamine-driven feedback loops we've created are destroying how society works ... I feel tremen-*

dous guilt. I think in the back, back recesses (of our minds) we knew something bad could happen ... Facebook is eroding the core foundation of how people behave by and between each other. My solution is using these tools only for that which is vital and that's as far as it goes.

The behaviour Palihapitiya is referring to is a loss of empathy, and a deepening sense of isolation as the world around us becomes less real the more addicted and dependent we become on our little highs. So, don't go anywhere near your smartphone, computer or any other gadget that has social-network sites on it first thing in the morning. And avoid watching the news first thing too because it's probably going to be death and destruction and negativity, and you just don't need that kickstarting your day.

EXERCISE: WHERE'S MY PHONE?

Get in the habit of not having your phone in your bedroom when it charges overnight. Leave it in the kitchen, or the living room, or just outside the bedroom door if you use it for an alarm clock. Or, if you're in a bedsit, hide it away in your bag. Trust me, you will sleep better when you go to bed, you won't be tempted to look at it during the night, and you won't be able to use it first thing. Write down a promise to yourself here, identifying the new location of your phone overnight.

I promise to keep my phone

_____

_____

_____

_____

_____

_____

BREATHING

'Breathe half, live half!'
– Stig Avall Severinsen

Breath is the very essence of life, it's why we can live on this planet, and yet many of us don't pay particular attention to the way we breathe, or how it affects us when we breathe properly. One of the first things that happens when we're nervous or stressed is our breath shortens and our inhalations become shallow to the extent that we're only taking in 30 per cent of the air we usually would if we were feeling grounded and unthreatened. The impact of this is that we pump less oxygen to the brain and in doing so lose our normal mental dexterity, which makes us produce more of the stress hormone, cortisol.

I'd gotten myself into such a bad way with alcohol and anti-depressants before I left Baghdad that I wasn't doing any exercise. Just drinking heavily, smoking, doing everything I could do that was self-harming. I was on a destructive path, consciously making the decision to get hammered, and as a result having regular anxiety attacks. I'd never experienced anything like that in my life before. There were moments when I thought I was dying, I couldn't breathe and it felt as if my body was closing down. I didn't understand what was happening to me, and I really thought that I was going to end up in a mental hospital and left there because I was clinically insane.

The solutions to every problem are within us, even for something as violently traumatic as a panic attack. In these moments, you must remember to breathe. It's all about pulling yourself back from the flames of hysteria to stillness, and breathing is the quickest rebalancer and antidote to panic. Breathing is everything.

In moments of absolute mayhem in your head, there's so much information for your brain to take in, and this is where you need to create a moment to debug, a pause. That means creating a gap. If you find yourself in a highly charged situation, before you start to focus on the one or two things that really matter, breathe for at least four inhalations and exhalations. The renewal of breath allows us clarity and thought. We then understand what it is that we've got to focus on. Triaging the situation is looking at the priorities that really matter and getting rid of all the gunk that doesn't. What can I control in this moment?

EXERCISE: BOX BREATHING

In the Special Forces in a number of countries, they teach 'Box Breathing', a means of centring the nervous soldier and calming the mind to achieve the best performance. This simple technique can be used by anybody and applied at any time and in any place, be it before an interview you might be feeling anxious about, making a speech or presentation, when you are forced into a pressured situation, or as a means of meditation.

Step 1: Inhale deeply through your nose for four seconds.

Step 2: Hold for four seconds.

Step 3: Breathe out through your mouth for four seconds.

Step 4: Hold for another four seconds.

Repeat four times and allow this pattern to form a more regulated and structured breathing cycle. Practise regularly and it will become less forced and engineered. Not only that, it will keep cortisol at bay and allow you to approach all matters with a more relaxed and clearer frame of mind.

MEDITATION

Meditation allows you to reach a state of stillness in yourself, a moment's peace. Once in that relaxed state, you can start to focus your attention at an intention you want to realise and consciously develop it. It's about clearing away all the mental garbage and endless chatter of those 100,000 thoughts racing around your brain on any given day. Sometimes while meditating, I drift away on a train of thought and then have to bring myself back to the meditation and recentre my mind as it's so easy for me to get distracted.

Meditation starts with observing your breath, the feeling of the air passing through your nose as you inhale, the rise of your chest as it fills with air, and then the slow exhalation of that breath. To do yourself justice you'll need to find somewhere quiet and something comfortable on which to lie down, like a yoga mat. The word 'inspire' derives from the old Greek word *inspiro*, meaning 'to breathe life into'. And this is what we're doing when we observe this fundamental function of ourselves. Breath connects us to the world around us and centres us. When you practise box breathing with your eyes closed and just focus on the breaths, it slows your heartbeat and immediately starts to relax your emotional and physical state.

Meditation (my surfer pals tell me) is like surfing in that it takes practice to get in your flow. If (unlike me) you're a competent surfer, you ride a wave without thinking about it, subconsciously changing your feet's position on the board in order to control it. Paddling out on a rough sea, constantly ducking under whitewater mush that's trying to take you all the way back to beach, can be soul-destroying for the beginner. Learning to read waves and wait for the interval between sets so you can paddle out beyond the impact zone is hard-won knowledge and to get there you must go through the painful learning process.

The problem with human beings is we want the low-hanging fruit, we want quick results without doing the hard work. I may want to be able to surf waves like Kelly Slater without doing any practice. What's more frustrating is the fact I know exactly what I've got to do to be of a decent standard, I understand the process required. But before I can glide like a bird across that blue wall of glass I need to start with the basics of learning how to pop-up off my board and position myself in the right place to catch the peel of the wave. The same can be said for meditating. It's possible you'll find it tricky to relax, lying on your back wondering what the hell you are doing to start with, but in a short space of time meditating becomes a trusted route to relaxation, and an oasis for the self where we can regather our energy and centre ourselves to be open to the gifts each new day has in store for us. Meditation not only helps us reduce stress, but improves our concentration, increases self-awareness and keeps us in the present; it's also good for promoting mental and physical well-being and induces happiness.

While I was a serving member of the Special Forces we were surrounded by chaos every day. Fortunately, we had systems, processes and routines designed to help deal with that chaos. Our minds were focused and controlled to deal with anything. My issues started when I left the Special Forces and I found myself bereft of these vital processes, and chaos ran riot in my life, both at home and in war zones. I found meditation out of desperation and it has been my friend ever since. It's curious that in the West we train our body so hard but fail to see how vital it is to provide the mind with the same level of maintenance. Until you're mentally prepared, you'll never be physically ready.

EXERCISE: MEDITATION

1. Set your alarm for ten minutes.
2. Begin box breathing, in for four, hold for four, out for four, hold for four. Concentrate on your breath, feel the air as it moves in and out of your body.
3. On the fourth breath as you exhale close your eyes, bringing your focus onto your breath.
4. As you control your breathing, focus on the future you want.
5. Anytime your mind wanders bring it back to the breath.
6. When you have a routine and your mind is clear, ask yourself the question: 'What is my number one goal?'

The initial focus here, and one that is ongoing, is the ability to clear our minds of distracting topics and scenarios and learn to focus. Once you can do this the benefits are obvious in everyday life. The mind chatter will fade and the clarity of thought will allow creativity to flow.

MIND AND BODY FOR LIFE NOT FOR LOOKS

The benefits of physical exercise are endless for both the body and the mind. Every time you exercise:

- You're showing respect to your body, telling it you care, which is good for your self-esteem
- Endorphins are produced by the brain which make you feel more positive. They also aid your memory and make you feel mentally sharper
- Increases motor skills, ease of movement
- It boosts self-esteem (at my lowest in Brisbane it picked me up despite my lack of purpose in the oil company)
- Helps you sleep
- Improves bone strength and builds muscle
- Gives you more energy
- Helps you lose weight
- Improves your immune system
- Aids digestion and speeds metabolism
- Boosts your sex drive
- Reduces stress and anxiety
- Helps lessen depression
- Helps fight Alzheimer's
- Lessens the symptoms of Parkinson's
- Fights addiction cravings by providing you with dopamine, the reward chemical associated with sex, drugs and alcohol
- Increases relaxation

The average adult should be doing between 75 and 150 minutes of exercise per week, be it moderate exercise like walking or cycling or more strenuous like running, swimming, yoga, spin class, aerobics, skipping, boxercise, football ... I could go on! Basically, anything that gets your heart going quicker than it usually does. Looking good should be a by-product of exercise not the be all and end all. It's about feeling good on the inside.

Exercise formed a vital part of my recovery from alcohol abuse and kept me on the straight and narrow to fulfil my goals. The best kind of exercise is that which gives you a cardiovascular workout. My morning run during bootcamp and to this day is always alternated by a circuit of exercises.

The best exercise is that which takes you outside in the elements. It's here that the soul is healed and your lungs fill with fresh air. If you're running or doing some form of workout in a park or the countryside, reconnecting with nature clears your head and sets the mind free creatively. Many find their best ideas come while exercising. Certainly that's the case with me. When we stay inside our houses it's as if we're boxed in, limited by their dimensions. Outside, nature is full of abundance, there is space and energy that fuels the mind giving it the medicine it needs. Interestingly, mental illness shares the common trait of keeping their victims prisoners inside.

Everybody has different fitness levels they start at so it's pointless me suggesting a mean average here, but a morning routine might consist of jogging, press-ups, stomach crunches, squats, burpees and short sprints. Find your own limits and slowly build them up. It's better to do two sets of 15 burpees than 30 burpees at once and tire yourself out or pull a muscle. Take it slowly; life is a marathon not a sprint.

EXERCISE: I DON'T LIKE RUNNING

If running isn't your bag, a good way to get into it is to run 50 paces then walk 100 paces. Over a period of time slowly increase the running count to say 100, while at the same time reducing the walking to 50.

Gradually increase your running duration and number of sets and keep a record of your progress. Just looking at your success gives you the encouragement you need to keep going.

When we become depressed one of the first things that goes out of the window is exercise and watching what we put into our bodies. So when our input of healthy food and exercise stops it has a direct effect on our output. No wonder we can't achieve much when we're blue, for our self-esteem falls, as does our motivation, our energy levels and sense of get-up-and-go. We gravitate to old habits of lazy eating, scoffing chocolate in excess, fatty foods, crisps, ready-made meals that take a few minutes to cook in a microwave and require no prep or finessing, takeaways … and our five-a-day ends up being rather less. So more calories and no exercise adds up to us putting on more weight and feeling bad about ourselves because we've abandoned ourselves to neglect.

Fitness for me has always been a major part of my life; I ran cross-country to keep out of trouble as a teenager; I ran my way into the Marines; while as an elite combat frogman of the Special Boat Service I had to be super-fit in the water and out of it too. And in Brisbane I was running from my demons. These days I need to exercise, not only because part of my TV job requires me to climb up moving boats, jump out of airplanes, scale cliffs – you know the stuff we sometimes do on *SAS: Who Dares Wins*, but also for Break-Point as much of what we teach is physical-based. Exercise helps me maintain an even keel mentally. There is nothing better to pull yourself out of a pit of despair than getting out in the fresh air and natural surroundings, it has an instant curative effect on the soul and the body.

Because of the pressure social networks place on us cosmetically speaking, we're more in the spotlight than ever. At the press of a button a picture of us on holiday looking our best can suddenly be seen by thousands of people; no wonder our vanity, which is hardwired to our ego, has never been quite so overblown, or so disproportionately important. Many of us are prepared to sacrifice feeling for perception, and instead of focusing on the way we look and experiencing life from the outside in – i.e., lots of Instagram likes appealing to our ego which make us feel good with little dopamine rewards – we should live life from inside out, doing exercise that makes us feel good within ourselves, for an inner smile radiates to a happy being on the outside too. After all, if we live a life based on looks, what have we got to look forward to in old age? Shame and regret for no longer being what we once were? Everything starts on the inside and radiates outward. Keep fit and embrace your years and wisdom; you're not supposed to look like a teenager at the age of 45.

You only have to look at those Hollywood faces we grew up with (not mentioning any names) but there are those who have grown old gracefully with laughter lines or handsome cragginess and have kept their natural shape, and there are those who try to look like the person they think everybody loved back in the day. The latter end up resembling frozen mannequins with no expression in their faces, while the former who are happy on the inside don't measure their self-worth by how many people say they look amazing, beautiful and not a day older.

If you're exercising simply to look great and reduce your body fat down to zero, rather than exercising to feel great, you're missing the point. Being healthy and fit is not about punishing yourself in the gym so you look like a statue, rather it embodies mind, body and nutrition: well-being through taking care of the mind, exercising the body and eating food that is good for you. Mindfulness, the Stoic practice of consciously ignoring negative thoughts and focusing on positives, is at the bedrock of everything I do. If you can't weed out negative thought patterns and quieten the self-doubting judgemental, ego-based you, you'll always be living on the outside.

A great deal of research has been conducted into what helps to create a peak athlete and there's one common denominator they all have: a positive mindset. Mental attitude has a massive effect on your fitness goals. According to research on positive psychology, there are four key areas in our lives we must meet. How many of these would you say were true to you?

- **Positive subjective experience:** How in flow with ourselves we are, how happy we feel, expressing gratitude for what we have in our life and realising we are blessed with abundance rather than lack.
- **Positive individual traits:** Being kind to ourselves, recognising our talents, hobbies and positive elements of our character.
- **Positive interpersonal relationships:** Having a positive, supportive tribe around us, where there's a two-way street of give and take, is reassuring and inspiring.
- **Positive institutions:** Being part of a team or a club creates new friendships and better social bonds, as well as organised processes to help us achieve our physical goals.

NUTRITION

You can train as hard as you like but you can't out train a bad diet! This is where so many people fall down – including me. We *think* what we eat. The food we eat can promote the repair of tissue in the brain, control hormones and aid neurons that transfer information to our body. Food directly affects mood, so we *are* what we eat. This year (2020), depression will rank as the second highest cause of disability after heart disease, and the chances of becoming depressed are a staggering 80 per cent more for those whose diets are full of processed food high in saturated fats, compared with people who eat whole foods. Ninety per cent of the body's serotonin, its feel-good chemical, is in the gut, and is activated by eating the right food. You can dictate how you feel on the inside – sprightly or slothful, happy or fed up – by what you eat.

Your brain is always on. It takes care of your thoughts and movements, your breathing and heartbeat, and your senses, working 24/7, even while you're fast asleep. This means your brain requires a constant fuel supply. That 'fuel' comes from the foods you eat, and what's in the fuel makes all the difference. What we eat directly affects the structure of our brain and mood. Like a highly tuned sports car, our brain functions best when it is fed premium fuel, and that means high-quality foods containing plenty of vitamins, minerals and antioxidants which nourish and protect it from oxidative stress, the waste (free radicals) produced by the brain when the body uses oxygen. Just like an expensive car, your brain can be damaged by low-premium fuel like processed or refined foods. Diets high in refined sugars are damaging to the brain and can hamper your body's regulation of insulin and promote inflammation and oxidative stress. Multiple studies have found a massive correlation between a diet high in refined sugars and impaired brain function, and even a worsening of symptoms of mood disorders, such as depression. What's interesting is that the medical establishment, for many years, did not acknowledge the connection between mood and food.

I've tried all kinds of eating disciplines from paleo to vegan and have now come to a balance in my life that doesn't put me under pressure when I'm travelling or in a rush. It's about making conscious choices and there are certain things I simply will not eat. Many people claim to be vegan, but the fact is most of them are not, they're just making better choices of what they eat and are choosing more of a plant-based flexitarian diet. Like me.

I rarely eat red meat and will usually opt for fish over chicken. And if I do decide to have steak and chips, I don't beat myself up about it. The things I do steer clear of, however, are processed foods and dairy. Humans are the only species that drink the milk of other animals. Seventy-five per cent of the world's population are lactose- (the main carbohydrate in milk) intolerant, which can cause digestive problems, nausea, vomiting and diarrhoea. I also make the choice to buy organic over non-organic foods. The way I see it is that non-organic food has had chemicals and pesticides on it to keep insects away. If the insects wouldn't eat it then why would you? True, you're a lot bigger than an insect, but the amount of non-organic foods we eat over a long period increases the chemical percentage that affects your body and brain; increases in weight, skin irritations and inflammation soon follow, for you have long been creating the right environment for disease and unrest in your body.

MOOD FOOD

Here's a list of foods that keep your brain healthy and on-point, not that you need stick to only this menu for the rest of your life!

Fatty fish – When people talk about brain food, fatty fish is often the top of list. Think salmon, trout and sardines, all of which are rich sources for **omega-3 fatty acids**. About 60 per cent of your brain is made up of fat and half of that fat is the omega-3 kind. Your brain uses omega-3s to build brain and nerve cells, and these fats are essential for learning and memory, as well as warding off age-related mental decline, and quite possibly keeping Alzheimer's at bay. One study found that the brains of people who ate baked or broiled fish regularly, had more grey matter – which contains most of the nerve cells responsible for decision-making, memory and emotion – than those who didn't.

Coffee – If coffee is the highlight of your morning, then you'll be glad to hear it is good for your brain as it contains **caffeine** and **antioxidants**. Caffeine increases alertness, sharpens concentration and may also boost serotonin levels. One study found that when participants drank one large coffee in the morning, or regular smaller amounts throughout the day, they were more effective at tasks that required concentration.

Blueberries – Blueberries and other deeply coloured berries deliver **anthocyanins**, a group of plant compounds with anti-inflammatory and antioxidant effects, for both oxidative stress and inflammation are likely key contributors to brain ageing and neurodegenerative diseases like Parkinson's. Some of the antioxidants in blueberries have also been found to accumulate in the brain and help improve communication between brain cells.

Turmeric – This deep yellow spice has generated lots of buzz. As well as being a key ingredient in curry powder, it contains the active ingredient, **curcumin**, which is able to cross the blood–brain barrier and have a positive effect on the cells there. It has been linked to increased memory for people with Alzheimer's, as well as boosting serotonin and dopamine, respectively mood and energy chemicals within our brains that keep depression at bay. One study found that curcumin improved depression symptoms just as efficiently as an anti-depressant, over a six-week period. Curcumin is also an antioxidant and anti-inflammatory.

Broccoli – One small cup of broccoli delivers more than 100 per cent of your RDI (recommended daily intake) of **vitamin K**, the vitamin responsible for helping blood clotting, bone metabolism and regulating blood calcium levels. It is also an antioxidant and anti-inflammatory.

Pumpkin Seeds – Containing powerful antioxidants that protect your body and brain from free radical damage, pumpkin seeds are an excellent source of **magnesium** (essential for combatting depression, epilepsy and other neurological diseases, and aiding memory and learning), **iron** (fights brain fog and impaired brain function), **zinc** (crucial for nerve-signalling and helps deter neurological diseases like Alzheimer's and Parkinson's) and **copper** (again low levels of copper can lead to neurodegenerative disorders like Parkinson's and Alzheimer's).

Dark Chocolate – Dark chocolate and cocoa powder are bursting with brain-boosting compounds including **flavonoids**, which may help protect the brain slow down age-related mental decline as well as aiding memory. Chocolate is also a legitimate mood booster.

Nuts – Eating nuts may prevent coronary heart disease, support the immune system, promote eye health, aid brain cognition, and lower the risk of cancer, thanks to them containing **vitamin E**, a fat-soluble nutrient, and antioxidants. Vitamin E shields cell membranes from free radical damage, helping slow mental decline. Walnuts may be the best nuts for your brain as they also deliver omega-3 fatty acids.

Oranges – Your RDI of **vitamin C** can be achieved by consuming just one orange. Vitamin C is known to fight age-related mental decline and is a powerful antioxidant that helps fight off free radicals which can damage brain cells. You can also get excellent amounts of vitamin C from strawberries, kiwi, tomatoes, bell peppers and guava.

Eggs – Containing several nutrients that are tied to brain health, eggs contain vitamins B6 and B12, folate and choline. The latter is key to memory and fluid mental function. The egg yolk has the most concentrated source of this nutrient. Folate deficiency is common among elderly people with dementia, and studies show that folic supplements can help minimise age-related mental decline, while B12 helps synthesise brain chemicals and regulate sugar levels in the brain.

Green Tea – Green tea is an excellent drink to support your brain, performance, memory and focus, while its antioxidants protect the brain. Also present in green tea is L-theanine, an amino acid that can cross the blood–brain barrier and increase the activity of the neurotransmitter GABA, which helps reduce anxiety and helps you relax.

Water – Given that our bodies are made up of around 65 per cent water, it's amazing that we struggle to drink enough to filter the toxins from our bodies and keep it functioning correctly. Equally we don't pay enough heed to where the water that we drink has come from. I distil all my water in order to reduce the level of unnatural chemicals going into my body and brain. In drinking filtered water you're avoiding potentially harmful contaminants like pesticides, viruses and herbicides that can be present in tap water. Drinking plenty of water can help reduce kidney stones, eradicate constipation, and help protect your teeth.

PART IV

HOW TO SUSTAIN CHANGE

CHAPTER 12

DEALING WITH FAILURE

IF YOU DERAIL, GET BACK UP, SMILE AND CARRY ON

It's natural that on your way to achieving your goals, you'll make a series of failures or mistakes en route. If not, then your goal was too easy and you need to find a more challenging one. But rather than see these blips as stark failures, we should see them as milestones of growth. It's only a failure if you don't learn something useful from it, so you can avoid doing the same in the future. Sometimes a failure is a hidden blessing and exposes your goal as being impractical, causing you to stop (breathe), rethink it through (recalibrate) in order to smash it (deliver).

It's also the way you choose to frame what might at first seem like a failure but in fact turns out to be something different when viewed from an alternative angle. In 2017 I was approached to take part in a Special Forces boxing match for charity. I'd done a little kick-boxing as a kid but had never trained as a boxer, so I agreed on the condition that my opponent was pitched at the same level of inexperience as myself. I managed to raise £11,000 of sponsorship and as the event approached I took to the training with dedication. I was on the bags and sparring four times a week, in fact I had former-professional boxer Ross Minter as my coach, so I was taking it very seriously. Halfway through the training some intel arrived in our camp about the opposition – unbelievable, the guy I was fighting was a mixed martial arts (MMA) fighter! We responded that this wasn't on and trusted the organiser's word that they would sort it out. Come the night before the fight and we discovered they had made no attempt to change my opponent, I was still boxing the Navy-Seal-turned-MMA-fighter. To hell with it, I thought, I'd fight anyway; I was Battle Ready, fit as a fiddle and couldn't care less how much experience he had. But most importantly, I didn't want to let the charity down who I'd raised £11,000 for by cancelling the fight.

When the bell for the first round clanged, I was straight out of my corner and all over him like a cheap suit. I wasn't scared. And then his experience prevailed. He saw his window of opportunity as my guard dropped and out of nowhere he threw a blinder that caught me on the chin and dropped me like a stone. And that was the end of that. It's not called the 'Sweet Science' for nothing, it takes time to nurture your craft, put your cluster punches together, learn to counter-punch and protect yourself with your guard. I was an undergrad to say the least. My learning from the experience? It wasn't all about winning. I had gotten very fit in the training leading up to the fight and I had also enjoyed the discipline involved as I worked toward a specific goal and a specific date; I got to work with a kick-ass trainer who taught me the rudiments of a brilliant craft and most of all, I raised quite a lot of money for a good cause. Maybe I lost the fight to a better boxer, but there were quite a few wins too.

Getting to your goals can be like a game of pinball: accept that you're going to get knocked side to side on the way there, that's par for the course. Sometimes you can get knocked all the way back to the start again, but try not to view it as such, for on your second attempt you're gifted with wisdom you didn't possess on the first. The clearer your goal is and the more you want it, the more you can handle being knocked about to achieve it. You must be as bombproof as possible if you don't want to end up in the hurt locker licking your wounds and picking up the fragments of your broken dreams.

When I was getting dry during my three-month bootcamp in Cornwall, I didn't go to Alcoholics Anonymous meetings to help keep my resolve as I didn't consider myself an alcoholic. I wanted to have the choice to drink the odd pint. But without AA I lacked a constant scaffold of support around me, or a sponsor I could call when the banshee started wailing for her drink at 3 a.m. I knew that the control of anything was within me and as I had proof and experience of great feats of mental strength throughout my years in the Special Forces, I had the minerals to do what I needed on my own. Maybe this was also me being stubborn. I had gone to AA once before many years ago and had the opportunity to share – which I did – only to realise my drinking was merely child's play compared to most people in the room. The thing is it's all relative, and for me alcohol was holding me back from my full potential even when in a manageable state.

There were times after the bootcamp when admittedly I fell off the wagon, but over time drink became easier and easier to let go of. One such lapse was the day before filming series one of *SAS: Who Dares Wins*. My first day on set was a nightmare, my head was all over the place. I'm sure no one else noticed I wasn't 100 per cent but I did, and that's all that matters. I knew that I wasn't firing on all six cylinders and could be better, much better than I was. So, when it came to series two, I told myself, 'Right, in the next series I'm not going to be that person again. I'm going to give myself a chance to be the best version of myself.'

I made a verbal contract with myself: 'For the whole eight weeks leading up to and including the filming in Ecuador, I'm not drinking.' And I got through it. When it came to the wrap party, which promised to be as full-on as a bunch of thirsty Vikings freshly arrived in Valhalla, I managed to temper my temptation and old triggers from getting me back on the sauce. While Foxy was gearing up for a legendary session, I said, 'You know what, mate? I'm going to pass; I feel brilliant as I am.' Again, yet another break-point moment, a sliding door of opportunity.

It would have been so easy to do what I'd always done, with that self-serving egoic voice reassuring me, 'Yeah, you deserve this now. You've done really well, it's time to get absolutely wankered!' By just taking that moment of pause, of being aware of the lack of purpose of me drinking again, and the consequences that lay waiting for me, and instead responding to myself with, 'Look how good you feel. Why would you want to lose this?' I managed to flip my thinking. My 'inner me' was starting to blossom, the deeper self who could see beyond the ego. My reward for abstinence was that I woke up the next morning to a beautiful Ecuadorian dawn, and saw the sun rise while everyone else was still mothballed in hangovers. It felt amazing having broken that cycle.

Kicking alcohol was a major achievement for me and a significant step in my evolution as a person. Given the grip it once had on me, I never thought I'd be strong enough to pack it in, but once I conquered that, I realised that I could change anything in my life. Knowing I was in control was such a massive growth point for me. Everyone around me said, 'You'll never stop drinking!' and even I had told myself this having tried to be teetotal so many times before. But I conquered it, and even if I have had an occasional beer now and again, having found the stop mechanism I now know I can activate it whenever I need to. To reprogram the software we apply to our lives we have to look beyond what we think we're capable of. One of the ongoing side effects of my drinking, my relapse, was the feeling of guilt and shame. And guilt and shame are fuel to addiction.

WHAT CAUSES RELAPSE INTO OLD HABITS?

We are naturally wired to cling to the familiar, as explained in the Survival Blueprint. It can be any number of things that trigger our return to bad habits, be it exposure to places, people, boredom, emotions or things that trigger old behaviours because they trigger something in your brain and remind you of your old habit, which then gives rise to cravings. The first concession you have to allow yourself when you lapse and take a drink is that most of us waver in the early stages. You'll feel humiliated and tempted to throw in the towel. Try and reframe the setback as something you can learn from rather than be beaten by. See the relapse not as a return to the start but rather as a stage of your recovering your sobriety, gradually bringing you closer to achieving your goal. It's an opportunity for growth, not the beginning of the end; chances are you will be even more determined to commit to your goal the next time round.

So, cut yourself some slack, be kind to yourself, accept yourself and look for the positives. If you're sober 98 per cent of the time, don't focus on the 2 per cent you're not.

PLAN FOR THE WORST, AIM FOR THE BEST

The American astronaut Chris Hadfield in his book *An Astronaut's Guide to Life on Earth* describes how at NASA they negatively plan for the worst which gives them confidence. How so? Because space is an unforgiving place to make mistakes, so if you prep a contingency for every possible eventuality you can think of, you're more Battle Ready to deal with things if something goes south. If you already have solutions up your sleeve, you can relax. He believes it's about sweating the small stuff, learning about all those little things that could develop into something major. He asks, 'What's the next thing that can kill me?' Hadfield thinks that you can't control what life throws at you, but you can control how prepared for it you are.

THE FIVE-SECOND RULE

I like to read a lot, although I have to admit I have many unfinished books in my bookcase. Podcasts are another great resource and I recently came across Mel Robbins, a lawyer and the creator of the concept of the 'five-second rule'. Her message resonated with everything Break-Point stands for and really resonated with me too. Our enemy, she says, is the 'f' word – no, not that one! – *fine*. That's it, fine. On the surface it looks harmless, however when we say/think that fine is enough we're selling ourselves short. Fine is not enough, we deserve so much more. We all have life-changing ideas, but we do nothing about them. Mel Robbins calls it 'hitting the inner snooze button' and going back to sleep. In any area of our life that we want to change we are never going to feel like it. The propulsion required from being on autopilot to doing something new, she calls 'activation energy'.

Robbins and her husband were in financial debt after pouring all their life savings, home equity and kids' college education fees into a failed pizza business. Feeling helpless it seemed too big a problem for Robbins to solve. She found her only solace in sleep, at least until her alarm went off and then she'd be wide awake plagued by her thoughts. All she had to do was get up, make her kids breakfast, then look for a job, but that was too much for her.

Every night she made noble plans that the new day would be better and things would change; no more dread and fear. But every time the alarm went off she hit snooze and lay there defeated. Until one morning she counted 5-4-3-2-1 once the alarm went off and, mindful of watching a rocket taking off on TV the night before, launched herself out of bed. She realised that in that five seconds lay her road to recovery, because after that short span of opportunity the negative thoughts kicked straight in and kept her in bed. Following this success she began to apply the 5-second rule to many areas of her daily life and things began to improve very quickly.

Robbins says we should set our alarm thirty minutes earlier in the morning, and when it goes off, we have five seconds in which to jump out of bed. Once we climb out of a warm bed, we come face to face with the physical force required to change our behaviour. It's right at our fingertips, but instead we spend so much time waiting to be in the right mood to do something dynamic that we never get around to it. So, we must force ourselves through the short-term discomfort for the long-term gain. Imagine your brain as being made of two halves: autopilot and emergency brake. Anything that represents a new departure from your humdrum routine needs a level of will to make it happen as it will automatically receive an emergency brake from the brain.

'Force yourself out of your head. If you listen to how you feel when it comes to what you want, you'll never get it because you'll never *feel* like it.' Remember the five-second rule. You've got five seconds before your brain starts to talk you out of getting up and your emergency brake is activated. Robbins teaches businesses to make quick intuitive decisions based on gut and instinct, rather than the intrusion of the brain and its danger-averse thinking. We know that the opportunity for growth and expansion lies in our ability to step outside of our comfort zone but *knowing what to do will never be enough.* Because of the way our brains are wired, when our thoughts and feelings are at war and when there is a conflict between what you know you should be doing and what you feel like doing, your feelings are always going to win. If you don't feel like doing it, you won't do it. If you have an impulse to act on a goal, you must physically move within five seconds or your brain will kill the idea.

Almost 2,000 years ago Emperor Marcus Aurelius was thinking along the same lines. In a daily journal he noted:

> *At dawn when you have trouble getting out of bed, tell yourself, 'I have to go to work as a human being. What do I have to complain of if I'm going to do what I was born for – the things I was brought into the world to do? Or is this what I was created for? To huddle under the blankets and stay warm?'*

When you have found your inner purpose and a goal to match it, getting up with intention is easier than you may think. If you have a goal of launching your own business and you have no idea where to start, get on Google right now and research other companies in your field of interest, see what they're doing and decide what you'll do similarly and where you'll differentiate yourself. Knowledge is the key to achieving your dreams. Then google a free business-plan template and fill it out. Get serious about it and put your intentions in writing.

Whatever your goals are, show the world and yourself that you're serious by taking action, however insignificant that action may seem, right now. Because when you physically move, your brain starts to build new habits. When you do something you're not used to doing, you are in the act of building new habits and erasing existing ones. You have to force yourself into action. Plan your week ahead, consider what might pop up as an obstacle and be used by your brain as an excuse. The reason the Special Forces have done so well is because of their ability to take the shot without having to seek the authority from command. Once you see the shot in your crosshairs, take it before the window of opportunity has passed; sometimes you have to trust your gut and take the plunge.

FEAR

In our blackest moments exist our deepest growth opportunities where we either perish or flourish. Through difficulty we learn who we really are. When the call to change comes, we are faced with a challenge that frightens us but could at the same time send our life in a more positive trajectory. In his book, *The Hero with a Thousand Faces*, Joseph Campbell believes we all have an inner purpose which calls to us at some time or other in our lives:

> *If you follow your bliss [your calling] you put yourselves on a kind of track that has been there all the while, waiting for you ... don't be afraid, and doors will open where you didn't know they were going to be.*

Fortune favours the bold, and when life opportunities present themselves, those prepared to leave the safe and familiar are amply rewarded. If we can embrace the unknown and keep moving, we become stronger, as it's in the darkness we create something new. Einstein once said: 'If you always do what you've always done, you'll always get what you've always got.' To change anything in our lives we must step away from the predictable when the call comes. To fulfil our potential, we need to confront our inner fears and, in the process, become fuller versions of ourselves. Fear left untreated creates a monster, and that monster just gets bigger the longer you leave it. It's only when you turn around and look into its eyes that your monster shrinks. So, by exploring our fear more intimately, we start to habituate ourselves to it and it loses its sorcery.

In a non-stressed state, our brains can handle four or five pieces of information at any one time, but when we get stressed it lowers to one or two. The first steps toward doing anything new are always the hardest, whether it's climbing into a boxing ring, scaling a mountain, or riding a horse, as with those first steps your mind will panic and the lizard brain will shut down your thinking brain and try and cripple you with fear. But keep going *another* couple of strides and fear's attempt to hold you back suddenly melts off you like snow on your shoulders in the bright sun ... and then you're moving on to fresh, exciting ground.

In the Special Forces I'd be in a four-man team piled up behind a door about to go into what was usually a shitstorm of the highest order, and it was one of the most stressful moments of my life. Imagine it, you've got your weapon ready and loaded, safety catch off, your heart drumming against your ribcage with anticipation. Then a hand on your shoulder gives you 'the squeeze' to inform you the guys behind you are stacked up and ready to go. You pass it on to the guy in front of you, and if you're second man in, that means giving the squeeze to the point man (first man in), at which juncture, it's time to rock 'n' roll and let rip the dogs of war. The stress and anxiety ramping up is hard to describe. What are we walking into on the other side of the door? A wall of bullets? A bomb? You never know until you're in the theatre, screaming bullets ricocheting from walls, bodies going down around you.

Fear never goes away and although it might not feel like it, fear is your friend; an emotional and mental rehearsal of what you don't want to happen. If we can learn to habitually think of it and observe it as such, it helps rein it in. Earlier in the book, I mentioned the term 'one-metre square', a resilience model the Special Forces soldier uses in an attempt to calm himself with a combo of box breathing and by blocking out everything else but the one-metre square around himself.

Given that fear is a part of who we are, however unhelpful it may seem in the twenty-first century when there are myriad problems seemingly flying at you from every frickin' direction, you need to counterbalance the panic with rational thinking and a process that keeps you from going directly to fight-or-flight response. Take it back to focusing on your breathing: each deep inhalation lowers your cortisol; each exhalation brings you better clarity. Sometimes it's a good idea to move around if you're sitting fixed at your desk. You may be frozen with panic or stress. The best antidote to this is fresh air and a walk; your energy will be completely different by the time you return to your seat.

Remember that the more processes you have built in to achieving your goal, the less vulnerable you are to the tricks your mind will try to play on you. Procrastination is something the ego and your survival blueprint will often use to hold you back when you approach a challenge, and the quickest cure for it is to trust your gut and push forward into action – the five-second rule should also be used when you're putting something off. Doing something, *anything*, is better than nothing. Look for the break point then act on it. And trust your instinct – science has proved there are as many neurons in our gut as a cat has in its brain, and cats are smart, so follow your hunches and take a leap.

In tight spots you either have a mind of clarity or a mind of confusion. When I was in that car being attacked by the militia, outnumbered, driving at 140kph with 12 people in vehicles in front dependent on me for saving their lives, I don't mind admitting that initially I was overwhelmed, the situation got hold of me, and was threatening to unravel everything. I breathed, took it back to one metre, remembered I was experienced and had trained for this, and that despite the odds I would control the situation and we would prevail. And I breathed all the way through the execution of what needed to be done reaching a flow state that allowed me to slow everything down and execute the necessary action, on my terms.

STIR THINGS UP AND RISK A REBELLION!

If you want to perform, then don't conform. You need to stir it up, do something different to wake yourself from slumber. I mentioned the brilliant scientist and bestselling author, Joe Dispenza in Chapter 5 on neuroplasticity. He believes most of us do the same thing every day, living our life by habit, and that we are programmed to repeat this lazy, predictable itinerary as if on a treadmill. It reminds me of *The Truman Show*, in which Jim Carrey's character begins to feel frustrated by the fact nothing ever changes in his life. Every day is identical, the same faces passing him at the same time. Comfortable it might look, but happy he is not. He suspects there's a bigger world out there and he wants to experience it, but even his best friend tries to talk him out of it.

In 'Unlock The Unlimited Power of Your Mind Today!', a YouTube conversation with Ed Mylett, Dispenza says: 'Most people are living their life through the lens of the past, *unconsciously*, and they are filling in reality from their past memory. In our perceptions we overlay our future, the present moment with our memory of the past. That then diminishes possibility and begins to close down the way that we can navigate and function in our lives.'

It's only when Truman starts being less like a predictable robot and more like a mischievous human that life gets interesting for him. It's as if he has suddenly woken up. When he questions the status quo and starts doing things differently he starts to become bigger than the mould he was stuck in. Dispenza goes on to say that it is only by making a decision with hugely forceful intention that we are able to challenge the hardwired programming in our brains and bodies and therefore change our perceptions about ourselves and our lives.

CHAPTER 13

LIFE, THE UNIVERSE AND EVERYTHING

TRUSTING THE INTELLIGENCE
OF THE UNIVERSE

Our mindset governs the way we look at the world. We need to shift our inner programming from operating from a place of fear to one of excitement and curiosity. Einstein put it beautifully: 'There are only two ways to live your life. One is as though nothing is a miracle. The other is as though everything is a miracle.'

In moments when our thoughts are free of anxiety it's like seeing the world with a fresh pair of eyes; life seems full of possibility and we feel more connected not only to ourselves but to the music of the Universe. Anything seems within our capability. At times like this we are in-flow, just as we were designed to be. We were born to feel connected to our world, not live in constant fear of it. The bubble of our inner happiness is always trying to burst free from under the water: it's the negative thoughts we allow ourselves to fixate on that hold it down. In order to access this happiness we need to be more in tune with our thinking and feelings – we need to become an observer of ourselves. For me, it starts with trusting we're not on this blue dot (perfectly positioned to the sun – scientists call it the Goldilocks Zone!) by accident, but are part of something infinitely bigger than ourselves, something much more in control and intelligent. And when we trust and submit to this benign force, life stops being quite so anxious and opens up into something more magical.

ENERGY IN MOTION

Our bodies are constantly replacing old cells with new ones at a rate of millions per second. By the time you finish this sentence, 50 million cells of yours will have died and been replaced by new ones. In a healthy body the lifecycle of every cell is controlled, so you should always have just the right number of each type of cell. Remember that statement, 'A leopard never changes his spots!' meaning people can't change, yet this is more rubbish passed down from the ages. We are energy in constant motion.

Thoughts and feelings are energy. In fact, every living thing possesses energy. Look back at the jobs you enjoyed compared to those you didn't; how much more effortless were the ones you liked, how quickly the day went by, and how productive you were, compared to the stop–start treadmill and poor levels of concentration in jobs where you were just going through the motions. When we do something we are passionate about it's almost as if it happens by intuition, a sort of magic is at work, an energy that flows from our fingers and being into what we are engaged with. We often refer to this as being 'in flow' or 'in the zone'.

Negativity is also energy and creates a surge of power in the body. Some people become addicted to this energy and are the Dyson vacuum cleaners of positivity and joy.

Whether it's sports, painting, writing, soldiering, or whatever you happen to be in flow with, you not only possess an aptitude for it but it also makes you feel good when you're doing it, and the act of concentration is less tiring. The work of a person with writer's block who hacks away at their story despite not feeling connected with it, is a very different read to one written by someone who loves his subject and is lost in his work; the first is forgettable and sterile, the second flows, its fluid sentences perfectly lifting the subject matter off the page.

BE WATER, MY FRIEND

William Blake, the visionary poet who liked to wander around in the buff, once wrote: 'The fountain overflows, the cistern contains', believing that energy that is contained will go stagnant and perish, while that allowed to flow freely is alive and expressive. Centuries later, Dr Masaru Emoto wanted to test if crystals from different sources of water all looked the same. He discovered that water from free-flowing streams produced stunningly beautiful and unique crystalline structures that looked like snowflakes, while polluted or stagnant water created no crystals at all, just irregular structures that were black and sad-looking. He took it a step further by playing gentle classical music and heavy-metal music to water, discovering that the crystals broke down under stress and noise, but flourished with calmness. Next, he photographed liberating water from a dam; what had looked like a cockle shell with an irregular surface reformed into an ice-white diamond-shaped crystal. Finally, he wrote words on a bit of sticky tape and stuck them to the different petri dishes containing water. Words like 'compassion' and 'love' produced fine crystalline patterns, while negative words like 'hate' and 'cruelty' produced the predictable malformed, dark structures.

To me this highlights just how powerful the energies we radiate are, and given that we are all 75 per cent water, then we need to think about the effect we are having on other people and be mindful of our thoughts, as thoughts generate feelings that produce corresponding actions. The way you feel about something or somebody governs the energy that flows from you to them. Obviously, if it's a positive feeling you experience in their company or when replying to their email, this will be communicated in your underlying energy. When two people meet and there's a block to this energy flow, when it gets stuck, one will often say of the other person that they didn't 'get them', or they 'gave off a weird vibe'. Their energies are just not vibrating together.

Relationships, family, work, and personal interests are our building blocks of happiness, and we must be mindful of the energy we bring to all of them. If you are channelling negative energy towards your job, for instance, constantly complaining about it, your experience of it will only get worse until you resign or are made redundant. Then there's the self-loathing when you get exactly what you've been thinking about. You're never going to enjoy the success you desire at work if you're constantly in a negative vibration with your job. The sooner we recognise that the energy we radiate changes the environment around us, the better. We are much more powerful than we realise.

In life, we manifest what we think and feel strongly about; positive energy begets positive results and negative energy begets … you guessed it. When we think about relationships, there are certain couples who will never gel together and produce symmetry and light, because their energies are in conflict and not in vibration or, as some put it, they are 'a square peg in a round hole'. A lot of people fear leaving a relationship because of their fear of the unknown, and so they end up existing but barely living in this unhappy energy. I was certainly guilty of this in my first marriage and it made me realise that you can't live your life based on someone else's happiness if you're not happy yourself. You must be selfish about what you want in life and shift your energy to something or someone that allows you to express yourself and be in flow with them.

Recently a girl who'd come on one of our Break-Point courses phoned me and said, 'I need to thank you.'

'Why?' I said.

'Well, after the course and reading your book, I left my husband.'

'Wow, is that a good thing?'

'Yes,' she answered, 'it is, because they made me question what I want in life, and it gave me the strength to be able to choose what I did and didn't want.'

She'd been courageous enough to embrace the opportunity of a new life: short-term discomfort for long-term gain.

Remembering Blake's quote on water, we should never sit on our laurels and be complacent with life, even when we have fulfilled our goals. Regardless of our situation, we should be continuous models of improvement, for we can always be more kind, patient and curious. Like people who stop taking their vitamins once they've attained a level of healthiness, I'm conscious of the fact that I've always delved into self-help wisdom when I was at a low ebb, and then as soon as I felt better I assumed everything was fixed and so stopped doing the things that fixed me in the first place. That's when you end up on the constant rollercoaster of life as you fail to be consistent in what defines your motivation in the first place. We should never stop observing ourselves and our thoughts, checking the ego is not steering us, meditating, and generally investing in ourselves.

Animals are satisfied because they operate within simple parameters. Humans, however, are limitless in their capabilities and should never be satisfied, because as soon as you're satisfied, that's when the rot sets in; if you're satisfied then you no longer have a purpose or goal. When fresh rainwater hits *terra firma* and forms a puddle, its energy, which has travelled miles on its journey from the clouds, goes stagnant very quickly. We humans are no different. And that's when disease, *dis-ease* starts, because there's no flow … no energy.

It's safe to say that water that has no motion at all will become stagnant and toxic, and it's the same with our bodies. Similarly, if you allow yourself to live in a state of anger, your body is in a state of dis-harmony, dis-ease. And that's when it's subject to more of the same, as you open yourself to negative energy and you become ill more often. Negative breeds only negative.

I've been in relationships that have gone sour, and I know when I start to think, 'Yup, I want to be somewhere else', the Universe will take me away from that at some point because I'm starting to visualise not being there. When you start thinking like that, your energy towards that person has changed; you might be there physically, but energetically speaking you're not there at all, you're more like a hollow ghost. When my marriage broke down, it did so with good reason: we weren't right for each other, and no matter what I might have tried, this harsh fact was never going to change. I was unhappy, restless and we brought out the worst in each other.

This probably explains why I repeated the pattern of my father when I left my wife and went off to Iraq, though for a long time before that moment I had been dreaming of not being with my first wife. I got what I asked for at the end of the day, and luckily, I met someone else – who was immediately blamed for the breakdown of our marriage – but in truth, the marriage was in ruins well before we met.

EVERYTHING HAPPENS FOR A REASON

Remember those dot-to-dot puzzles you did as a kid? At first glance they meant nothing, just random black spots against a white page, but then as you gradually joined them up a picture began to form. Just as in life, over time certain apparently isolated experiences gradually coalesce to form a narrative of meaning, and once you start to see the connections, those dots merge into explanations writ large and bright as constellations. Looking back at my life, those dark moments that at the time seemed unfair, pointless and due to bad luck, were part of my evolution (if only I'd known that at the time!). I've learned that the closer you get to your inner self, the easier it is to see these dots connecting together to form a reassuring and beautiful plan amid what to others seems like random chaos. Each time I felt lost, angry or depressed it was because the inner me knew I needed to be somewhere different, but in order to shift me, it produced these uncomfortable symptoms. The most important incident in my life is also the most disturbing thing that ever happened to me – yes, you guessed it, the chimp attack – and its reverberations continue like aftershocks from an earthquake up to this day.

So, remember there were three of us that summer day at the circus: me, my brother Justin, and my pal James? After the attack I lay there motionless like a ragdoll with the stuffing pulled out, looking up at the sky. Next to the horror-stricken circus worker who had found me was my friend James, his eyes wide with disbelief. He ran all the way back to my house to tell my mum what had happened. End of story (or dot, if you'll indulge me)? Fast forward a few decades to Afghanistan and my best pal Troy is a Colour Sergeant for Alpha Company, 40 Commando, desperately trying to requisition some new vehicles as many of their fleet had been blown up. He goes to the military transport officer, a bloke called Major Stafford at Camp Bastion and receives less than a warm welcome, in fact, he's all but thrown out of the office by the major, who randomly asks as he leaves, 'You wouldn't happen to know a Marine called Ollie Ollerton, would you?' Troy goes on to tell him he does, we're best mates, and then has the chutzpah to ask him why. It turns out the major is none other than my childhood friend James Stafford, who was witness to the chimp attack and has been trying to reach me for years after I'd disappeared and joined the Special Forces. Naturally, Troy got the vehicles he wanted!

Pure random chance or celestial design? There are many such 'coincidences' like this throughout my own story which make me believe there *is* a Universal intelligence at work, and the sooner we submit to its system and start to play by its rules, the sooner we can achieve whatever we want and lead fuller, happier lives. Everything happens for a reason, it just doesn't seem like that at the time. Admittedly, it's a hard pill to swallow when you're in the shit, things have gone south and somebody tries to comfort you with: 'There's a reason for this happening, you'll see.' 'Why? What's the point!?' our ego screams outraged.

When we begin to trust the process of the Universe and submit to its intelligence, the difficult moments life throws at us can be reframed as events sent to us for a reason. We have choice how we react: we can either feel targeted by life or learn from hard times, using them to grow into a better, wiser version of ourselves. The worst, most frightening of these dots for me was the chimp attack, but again when I look for the positives in that fateful afternoon, it proved to me at an early age that I possessed the necessary grit and strength within me to fight back at the moment of my imminent death. This experience, for all the shit that it subsequently threw up in my path, helped me succeed in passing selection for the British Special Forces, arguably one of the most physically and mentally punishing tests a person can submit themselves to.

I honestly believe everything happens to us for a reason, even bad times in our life are trying to teach us something, leading us to make a necessary change towards a more positive place. Sometimes someone is delivered to our path who will later bring us to that which we want, but at the time we're usually unaware of this because life is too busy happening around us to take pause. However, in hindsight, many personal meaningful coincidences – or 'synchronicities' – as coined by the Austrian psychiatrist, Karl Jung – have been happening throughout our life, even in times when we were stuck in a rut and didn't know things would get better.

If you're struggling to get your head around this idea of things being connected, let me tell you another little story. For as long as I remember, my best mate was a guy called Denny. We met him in Chapter 1 while I was in Brisbane. He'd always been my best mate and we'd got into a lot of trouble together. We'd speak sporadically when I was in Iraq, as he was there too. After I left, when I was living in Australia, he called me out of the blue one day and announced, 'I'm moving to Oz.' 'Whereabouts?' I said. It turned out he moved just down the road from me. That's a coincidence. And when I went to a party at his place, he introduced me to Simon.

When I met this guy, I realised within minutes of talking to him that he seemed familiar to me, and then it clicked – he was involved when I went through Special Forces Selection! But here we were on the other side of the world, in Australia, and many years later, and I'm being introduced to Simon, the guy that took me through my course. I was like, 'Holy fuck!' and he too was amazed at the mysterious synchronicity we were experiencing. All the hairs on the back of my neck stuck up like spikes on a pufferfish. There are around 7 billion people on the planet, and I just happened to bump into him!?

Because of Simon, I started working for the Grey Man, and in doing so began to rediscover myself. All these are stepping stones, dots that join to other dots to form that constellation or bigger picture that can only be viewed later with hindsight.

Consider the word 'coincidence' for a moment. What does it mean? Most dictionaries define it as a situation in which separate things happen by chance at the same time or in the same way. This doesn't really gel with my experience. It was more of a chain of events rather than two things happening at the same time. One person led me to another, who I'd already met on life's path, and through him a path opened up to my epiphany. When I examine this it still astounds me how magical the thread is that was shining all the while through my dark times. If only I'd known back then to trust it, that and the capability we all have of ordering from the Universe what we need, then I might not have been so despondent. The old adage, 'When the student is ready, the teacher appears' could almost be referring to the Universe opening itself up to us and revealing more of what we can achieve once we're ready in ourselves to start believing there is something at work much bigger than us. Interestingly the old Medieval Latin word *coin-cidere* translates as 'to fall together', which is what the dots do – they connect, even if they are separated by years or decades, to form a story and shine a light on our darkness.

EXERCISE: TRUST IN COINCIDENCE

Take a moment to look back on your life for coincidences. Write down people who have been instrumental in your success or happiness, when they came into your life and what led you to meet them. The more you start spotting these helpful leg-ups the Universe provides us with, the easier it is to trust the magic. In future don't brush it off, call it coincidence and forget it. Use this experience to question why it happened and ask yourself what does it mean? It may be nothing but more likely you're simply not connecting the dots.

Person:

_____

When did they come into my life?

_____

How did they help me? What insights did they help me reveal?

_____

_____

_____

_____

What led me to meet them?

_____

_____

WHERE YOU ARE IS WHERE YOU'RE SUPPOSED TO BE

So, if you're in a bad place at the moment know that you are on a journey with a path and however tough or unfair it might seem, by looking on your current hardship as something that can be learned from, you are taking the power back from it. Whether you've lost a loved one to cancer, your child is ill, or you have only weeks to live, even then there is a message we can take from the most difficult moments in our lives. You are exactly where you're supposed to be; our greatest breakthroughs often come from our biggest breakdowns. We have the freedom to choose how we respond and to relate to anything happening to us. We need to look at difficult situations in our lives and tell ourselves, 'This is paving the way for something new and exciting, the death of something old and the birth of something new.'

When something does come crashing down, and that might be the end of a relationship or a job, you've got to look back and ask yourself, 'What's my thinking been about this?' Because nine times out of ten, you've been thinking negative thoughts about it for a long time and you are simply getting what you thought about; if you feared the loss of it, you will attract the loss of it.

The critical moment of re-birth is also the most extreme moment of trauma and hell, because the old is going to try and take you down with it as it tumbles into the trash pit. For example, consider a toxic relationship you're trying to leave; once your partner realises they're not going to stop you, it can turn ugly. And this is a break-point moment, an opportunity to make a break for it, a pause in which you can either stay in your malnourishing 'comfort zone' and put an ineffective Band-Aid on it, or push through and upward to where life is trying to take you.

Remember: we weren't born to be miserable. There will be many little deaths in your life that you must let go of, giving way to new change. No wonder people who come out of bad relationships begin to blossom and do things that they've never done before. And remember, when any energy source is dying it will scream the loudest and fight to stay alive.

STOICISM

If you think the term 'stoic' means someone who just grins and bears the hardships of life but keeps going anyhow, you've got them all wrong. The Stoics of third-century BC Athens, and later still, the Roman stoics, were a wise and hardy bunch who believed that even though their fate was already predetermined they still possessed freedom in the way they were free to respond to whatever misfortune and good fortune was thrown at them. Very much like we saw with Viktor Frankl and his choice to remain kind and human in the Nazi deathcamps. The Stoics were also great planners who used to meditate on anything that could possibly go wrong in order that they could plan a contingency in the event of it actually happening. Instead of using the word 'failure' they substituted it with the word 'outcome'. And if an outcome was negative they tried to see it as an opportunity to learn something. To them your character and your reaction to blessings and misfortune was what mattered – accept the blessings without arrogance and treat the setbacks with level-headedness. The four pillars of stoicism are: wisdom, justice, temperance and courage. Not a bad bunch of mates to back you up in a firefight.

IT'S HOW WE FLIP A SITUATION
THAT DEFINES US

When life gets tough we have a choice, the experience can make us better or worse. Two thousand years ago, Roman Emperor, Marcus Aurelius, then the most powerful man in the world, sagely said: 'The impediment to action advances action, what stands in the way, becomes the way.' In other words, the obstacles we encounter are where the personal growth is; losing our job, flunking exams, being cheated on, are all grist to the mill. Stoics believed we could steer ourselves through the worst situations by focusing on what was in our control rather than worrying about things that were beyond our ability to change. The Stoic Epictetus made a list of 'Things within our control', and 'Things beyond our control'. In the latter he listed: job, parents, body, weather, economy, the past, the future, other people's actions, the fact we're going to die. And for 'Things within our control', he simply said 'Our beliefs.'

Many things that we think we can control, we actually can't. You can strive like hell for that promotion and do everything in your power to make sure it happens but ultimately the final decision is out of your hands. You can take great care of your health and respect your body, but again you have no control over an illness that may suddenly befall it. That's not to say you give in, the Stoics were a hardy bunch; rather what they were trying to say was no matter what situation we are in, we have a *choice* over how we react to it – our beliefs.

We can't control other people's reactions to us and the flux of what life throws at us, but we do have dominion over the way we respond to its challenges; we can bend with the wind. Epictetus believed our disappointment and frustration in life arises from thinking we can control things that are beyond our control, rather than focusing on what is within our control. It's a really useful way of thinking in a crisis: 'Okay, so I can't change this, but what am I in a position to do?' The Alcoholics Anonymous Serenity Prayer sums it up neatly: 'Give me the serenity to accept the things I cannot change, courage to change the things I can change, and the wisdom to know the difference.'

Aurelius maintained a diary to keep track of his moods and ingrain new trains of thought. It enabled him to see if he was being negative and also to map how successfully he counted his blessings and endeavoured to be positive. The idea of a journal which correlates sleep with mood, or what we're eating, to how active we feel is a great way of getting to know ourselves better. Seneca a first-century Roman politician and stoic, noted: 'Let us take note of what it is that particularly provokes us... Not all men are wounded in the same place; and so you ought to know what part of you is weak, so you can give it the most protection.'

EXERCISE: WHAT'S WORTH WORRYING ABOUT AND WHAT YOU CAN'T CONTROL

Write out a list of things that worry you and get you down; be it the state of the planet, the price of milk, your next-door neighbour's dog, your best friend's addiction, your lack of enthusiasm for your job... whatever it may be. It may be a long list.

Now make a second list from the first, but this time only include the entries you can control.

You'll see that there are actually very few things you currently worry about that you can control – be it the current ruling political party, your company's share-price dropping because of larger economic factors, possible traffic on the motorway, your boss's lack of empathy, or whatever. By accepting that there are things you just can't change, you start to let them go and immediately feel lighter. The one thing you have 100 per cent control of, the one person whose behaviour you can change, is you. Accept you can't control others, forget about things that haven't happened yet. When you reduce your list of worries you create more space for creativity and to focus on your priorities. This is essentially what being Battle Ready is all about – identifying the stuff that holds you back, dealing with it and getting on with your goals.

GIVING

When we park our ego and connect with our flow, our inner consciousness, something magical awakes in us. We stop thinking of ourselves and obsessions of what we need to make us happy and start to think of what benefit we can be to other people. Remember earlier I mentioned Viktor Frankl, whose book *Man's Search for Meaning* follows his horrific experience in Auschwitz? Even in situations of utter degradation, the spirit of humanity often shone through and Frankl noticed that those who survived were not the physically strong, but those individuals who were more interested in helping others than just focusing on themselves as victims. They had a purpose, a 'why', and it stoked their internal fire by being able to give.

When I started work for the Grey Man in South-east Asia, we infiltrated child-trafficking rings, saving many children destined for the sex trade. This was a major tipping point moment for me as I realised how much I loved helping others. Giving your time and effort to a cause greater than you, with no expectation of receiving anything back, is a wonderful feeling. I discovered I had a passion to help people lead happier, better lives using my own mistakes and the processes I put into play to turn them into positives. I almost feel selfish giving because what I get back outweighs what I put in. Society has encouraged us to become individuals rather than communities and somewhere along the line we've lost the value of putting others before ourselves. You only have to look at what is happening to our natural world to see an example of that selfishness.

The more we operate from a place of kindness and consideration for others, the more connected we feel to life. And the way in which we give also reflects the way in which we receive. It seems like the two things are opposite; however they're simply two sides of the same coin. Consider your response when somebody pays you a compliment. The chances are you feel embarrassed and have the urge to immediately reciprocate. This means you are struggling with the ability to receive and is a fundamental reason why you don't receive more of the things you really want. Getting into a practice of accepting and appreciating when someone gives something to us feels alien and, at times, rude. Next time this happens to you, understand that you are not the focus of the act, that focus should be on the person who is giving you that compliment. It's their moment, have some respect and don't ruin it. And if you're that one that's giving, don't allow recognition to be the purpose of the act. The fact is that the moment you are able to truly give and receive, your whole life opens up to abundance.

CHAPTER 14

RETURN TO
KONG ISLAND

'Soltara' is derived from the Spanish verb *soltar*, meaning to let go or release, and this is exactly what they do at the Soltara Healing Center: empower guests to bridge the gap between mind, body and spirit, and to cut ties with self-limiting beliefs, negative programmes and long-buried childhood trauma. The ayahuasca ingredients required for the special ritual in which the drinker is transported to their inner spiritual world, is said to have been introduced to an Inca king by King Solomon many thousands of years ago. How the synergy was discovered between the two components which make the brew – *Psychotropia viridis* shrub and *Basnisteriopsis caapi vine* – is unknown, though the taking of ayahuasca is first written about by Jesuit priests in Iquitos, Peru, in the 1700s.

The teacher plant shines an unremitting light of consciousness on the shadowed corners of our psyche, seeking out those hidden fractured fault lines in our subconscious that may have been troubling us for most of our lives. It doesn't matter whether they are buried deeper than the Mariana Trench, it will find them. We can only release these troubled areas of ourselves once we understand them, and to achieve this we need to confront them first. Not an easy feat ... returning to Kong Island to face my nemesis, I thought to myself.

Fortunately, the Soltara Healing Center, with its highly skilled and compassionate Peruvian Shipibo healers and facilitators, is adept at taking you through this short-term discomfort for long-term gain: combining the plant medicine ceremony with supportive embodiment practices and a unique integration programme that enables you to take the knowledge and lessons learned during your ayahuasca visions and put them into practice in your life back home. If I was going to brave the inner labyrinth of my troubled psyche, I couldn't have been in better hands; the Soltara Healing Center had decades-worth of combined experience working at top-rated ayahuasca retreat centres in the Peruvian Amazon.

We found the centre perched upon cliffs with uninterrupted views of the bottle-blue Gulf of Nicoya and backed by thick mountainous jungle, reminding me of an ex-drug cartel property. Ten veterans had come here for the treatment – Canadians, Americans, Australians and myself and Nicko – and we would join another eight civilians from all over the globe (mainly the US but a couple of people from the UK too).

Outside, the crickets were sawing relentlessly as we gathered in an induction room and were introduced to the programme. Over the course of four nights we would take the ayahuasca drink and we should come with an expectation of what we wished to explore, though '*la medecina*' (ayahuasca) would find its own path and give you what you needed, not what you wanted. Personally, I wanted to rid myself of the remains of my destructive behaviour, for though I had turned my life around I still feared the thought of finding myself back in the past. Like the chimp that haunted my psyche, I always felt as if my self-destructive behaviour was simmering just under the surface.

Upon our arrival and induction, we were introduced to the team and told what to expect over the coming days: a mix of debriefing sessions, discussions and workshops on integration back into society post-course. The staff were amazingly professional and possessed a very calming nature that made us all feel extremely at ease with the prospect of the dark journey ahead.

The first ceremony was called the *vomitivo* and took place the following morning, the day after our arrival. This technique, used by the Shipibo people to cleanse the body, stomach and intestinal tract prior to working with Ayahuasca, involves drinking many cups from a bowl of Herba Luisa (lemongrass) until the body naturally regurgitates it, or 'purges', to use the ceremonial term.

Early evening, the nearby jungle in a riot of noise, we met in the sacred *maloca*; a candlelit circular building with a thatched roof and open sides that aerated the breeze. At its centre were mattresses for the *curanderos* (shamanic healers), who would help us on our spiritual journey with the aid of interpreters, and at its periphery were 18 mattresses for us participants. After we had lain there in silence for an hour or so, the healers filed in, female and male Peruvians with faces that looked like ancient Incas. One by one we were invited to the centre to meet them and be administered the medicine.

Next, we were passed the ayahuasca drink – a darkly ominous brew – and told to hold it close to our lips, then close our eyes and state our intention. 'I open my body and soul, please rid me of this destructive behaviour,' I said quietly and drank it back. It tasted foul but I'd known far worse.

Candles were blown out, leaving the maloca in complete darkness, the nearby jungle pulsing with the calls of its inhabitants. I thought I could pick out the sounds of tree frogs, cicadas and the distant rumblings of wild pigs. Just as I was getting impatient for something to happen, with bodies variously retching and crying around me, *la medecina* kicked into overdrive. I was outside the cage of my mind and I couldn't get in. I sat up and opened my eyes but now I was *in* the cage and those bars keeping me prisoner had disappeared. The maloca was floating in the air like an Arabian carpet, I could even see underneath it, while the space around our narrow mattress, should we happen to fall out, was an infinite abyss. Geometric shapes started to form all around me, and I started reflecting on our humanity and what a pathetic bunch we choose to be at times, and how life can be so futile and pointless in respect of the things we get hung-up about and focus on. At the point when I thought this was the gateway to something more profound, the feelings subsided and left me in a state of confusion as to whether the medicine had worked at all, or whether it was just my overactive and creative mind in play.

I felt disappointed by the first ceremony, I'd expected so much more; instead I came away thinking that ayahuasca came along to say hello, introduced herself to me and left.

Ayahuasca, I'd read, induced terrifying visions, summoning long-buried trauma, releasing repressed emotions that could liberate its taker from dysfunctional behaviour and addiction; it gave you autobiographic visions, intuitive wisdom, the removal of psychological blockages through multiple perspectives; self-denials were exposed, your internal moral attitude was enhanced, there was a psychological restructure. That all sounded fine, better than fine. If even a quarter of that were to be true it would be life-changing. But so far, I was yet to be convinced.

Come the second night I was offered an increased dose – initially, it's important for the healers to gauge your tolerance to the drink so you're not thrown prematurely into something you're not mentally prepared for, if you could ever prepare for what lay waiting for you. Last night was an intended gentle take-off, but tonight's increased dose took very little time to propel me into the spiritual firmament, and I was back in the floating maloca. Geometric shapes encompassed my vision with increased intensity and I knew that this time ayahuasca was there to stay; well, at least for a little while. The healers started singing their beautiful *icaros* (healing songs) as they circulated round the room, stopping at everybody's bedside to draw out the badness from our bodies which they then spat into a bucket.

Figures retched over buckets while some giggled, others in tears, coiled up like embryos.

They say the *curandero* (Shipibo healer) can see in the dark, and that they can also see inside you. Listening to the female healer's beautiful singing was like a beautiful luminous bird that flew through the darkness to each and every one of us, bringing with every high and guttural note of that merciful song, pure reassurance. Add to this the feral snorts and chattering voices of the jungle and crash of the nearby surf, it was a wildly vivid experience.

SURRENDERING

To really get the best of ayahuasca they said you had to submit to the journey and *surrender* to the plant; a word you'll seldom find in most Special Forces soldiers' vocabularies. For me, getting into a state of surrender was hideous as I fought against the medicine taking over my mind and body, but I knew the medicine couldn't do its work while I was fighting against it. The ego plays such a massive part in the battle as it refuses to let go of its control over you.

When I finally gave into it that second night, the journey started with reflections and observations about my life and my character. I had a reflection of how much time all of us spend on being the person that isn't us, wasting precious energy on trying to project to others what we think we're supposed to be ... how happy we are, what a great time we're having, how picture-perfect our life is. I saw us as lifeless mannequins dressed to perfection yet void of emotion and humanity.

For me this falseness is amplified by the fact that on television I'm understandably stereotyped as a Special Forces soldier, but the disconnect between the perception of how I think and feel is so far from the reality. I'm just me, void of categorisation or label.

This was a massive reflection for me. We put so much energy into that person we're supposed to be, but it's the person in the shadows that is the real you, the one with his head in his hands with despair and depression. A person who cries, shows pain and suffering as well as courage and bravery. But so long as we look good from the outside, that's all that matters to us: living the Instagram lie. The result of trying to be this someone else we've put such energy into creating is that we become void of feeling, void of emotion. We are divorced from the real us and become a by-product of the 'false' us. We utterly rob ourselves. It was such a strong lesson.

My second major reflection that night was about judgement and how hard we are on ourselves. We put so much pressure on ourselves by being judgemental and self-critical. When we are critical of others this is truly an inner reflection of our own self-critic.

My thoughts then took me back to the circus and the chimpanzee that tried to kill me, aided by the vibrance and noise of the jungle. Over almost four decades since the incident, I'd never been able to muster a clear memory of the attack; I couldn't even focus on it, it was too deeply buried. That single moment one sunny day at the circus, had savagely ripped away any precious memories I held of my childhood before the attack, tossing them in the bin like unwanted candyfloss. Ten years of my life gone, amputated. But sitting on the mattress, I now started thinking about my recollection of the story and the way I relate it at speaking events; for the story is always focused upon me and the act of violence I was subjected to. Always from my perspective. I'm very much the victim, which is one thing we as humans do well in directing our energy towards, especially when we have lost the upper hand.

I was looking through the eyes of my ten-year-old self and could see the baby chimp at my feet. I cast my attention into the shadows from where the chimp had mounted its attack, waiting for the scenario to play out in ultra HD. But then a voice said, 'What about the chimp?' and my energy and focus immediately switched perspective. For the first time I saw the chimp from a completely different viewpoint. That poor animal had been chained up, and God knows, probably abused by its owners, and it was I who had entered the chimp's arena, not the other way around. I was the invader, the interloper. She didn't come hunting for me, she was just doing her thing, what she was supposed to do – defend her baby.

As I put myself into her mindset, I started to feel strange sensations throughout my body. When I looked up, I was no longer peering into the shadows, but looking into the harsh sunlight, my vision clouded with sunspots. But as I adjusted to the light, I could see an animal stood over my baby – a threat not only to my kin, but my species. I was looking at the boy and I had become the ... 'This is madness!' I thought to myself, managing to snap out of the morphing. For a moment I was able to put the brake on in my mind, holding back the craziness of what was happening as I tried to focus my thoughts elsewhere.

At this point I was sitting with my legs crossed, with one arm to the side supporting me. Then, without a thought for what I was doing, I scratched the top of my head with my paw and realised I was the picture-perfect vison of a chimp on a lazy sunny day! I hadn't escaped the madness at all, for there is nothing more futile than trying to outwit the truth plant; those all-knowing ayahuasca vines are like tentacles streaming through the darkness of your psyche and they will always find your futile boxed-up resistance, turn it upside down and shake it till the truth falls out.

I heard another voice in my head, speaking a word over and over to me that no soldier ever likes to hear: 'Surrender!' Again, my initial reaction was, 'Never!', but I knew in my bones that my defiance was pointless, and I opened the gates and accepted what was happening: my defences down, the student *finally* ready. Physically, I was now on my mat on all fours, my balled fists planted firmly into the mat, a primal rage coursing through my veins. I felt my ears, they were getting larger, my forearms bristling with fur. My back rippled with dense muscle, I let out an almighty roar signalling my imminent attack. I was becoming the chimp again, but this time a genetically mutated cyber-chimp, and in my eyes was a HUD (head-up display) reading 'INTRUDER. ENEMY', as if I was the Terminator.

I was so consumed by being the chimp I didn't attack the boy. In fact, the whole experience wasn't about the physical attack at all; it was about the emotion surrounding it from the chimp's perspective. This heightened sense of empathy and compassion led me to think about everything important in my life.

Laura, my girlfriend, would do anything to protect her son. I put her under pressure to keep the house tidy and also expected a lot from her in our business. I realised I was lacking compassion; that I wasn't her first priority, nor were work deadlines and the business, it was her son, William. Quite rightly, he was her most important priority, and she was only doing what the chimp had done, taking care of her kin. But now I realised she'd been doing too much, working hard for Break-Point and looking after William. In future, instead of harping on at her, I needed to pause and put myself into Laura's shoes. She was consumed by the business, it was suffocating her, ruling her life and leaving her precious little time for herself and William. I needed to be more compassionate and look to get her working less intensely on the business.

After a second dose drink of ayahuasca, the teacher plant took me to the highway in Iraq where we were ambushed by the Taliban. A level of guilt had always stayed with me since I shot the young kid who had been about to shoot me. I was in his vehicle now, looking through his eyes and I watched myself lift the weapon and shoot through the closed window as I was about to fire. It seemed I was applying the empathy I'd learned from the chimp to everything else that had been buried in my psyche. It gave me closure knowing that his intention was to open fire, it was just that the other guy in the white Land Cruiser (me) had the upper hand.

In the days that followed we had group sessions where we shared our experiences. I was worried my experience had been so profound it would belittle the stories of the group, and paranoid that it might appear that my ego was on fire (when it definitely wasn't). I needn't have worried; everyone else's stories were phenomenal. Although we were a mixed group, my focus was on the veterans, and it was incredible to see the tangled webs of trauma starting to unwind. This was so powerful and like no therapy I had ever heard of. The stories were traumatic, but you could see the work the plant was doing in allowing the trauma to be exposed and understood in a very profound way.

Following this, the second ceremony, we were given a night off in which to relax and reflect.

I was a little apprehensive as the third ceremony grew closer. I really hoped it wouldn't be a repeat of my turning into the ape, from which I'd gained so much insight, but given that I was nearing 50 and this trauma happened at ten years of age, I still had 40 years to work through. We went through the same process, as each of us took our medicine and set our intention, with a slight increase in the ayahuasca dose. 'I surrender my body and soul, please show my path!' I said.

I returned to my mat and shortly after, I felt the medicine taking control. When I opened my eyes, the geometry was so powerful, the sounds of the jungle defined, despite being mixed with the soundtrack of each of us variously reacting to our visions.

My first reflection was how outwardly judgemental we human beings are towards others, and how that in turn then creates so much self-criticism. We think there's this thousand-person audience following us around sabotaging all our efforts, when there isn't anyone. We put so much pressure on ourselves, create so many unnecessary situations. But once you let go of all that, you stop performing like an animal in a circus and become the real you. That night, as we were all locked in to our personal ayahuasca journeys, somebody started laughing hysterically and it set me off in fits of uncontrollable laughter; in fact, everyone started giggling, and it was lovely to hear, for it pulled us out of our visions and gave us pause to breathe and reset before heading back in. I felt incredibly connected to the other people; we'd all been through the pain and fear.

At this stage it was amazing and fun, and I almost felt like I was having a great experience. In fact, I could have spent the night in this state, but I was quick to remind myself, 'You're not here for the experience, you're here for the journey!' I then made my way back to the healers, took a second dose of ayahuasca and reaffirmed my intention.

I lay down, surrendered to the medicine, and the healers started to sing beside my mat. I was heading back to the circus and though that was the last thing I wanted, I realised that there was obviously still work to be done.

This time I became the ten-year-old me. I was being attacked by the chimp and fighting back. It was as I'd always told the story, sketchy, with no real noise or emotion, just me and the chimp. As I looked up at her gnashing teeth, I realised I was giving her what for. It was a proper scrap, a last-man-standing type event.

Then, like a human DVD player, I freeze-framed the action and asked myself, 'What if you had surrendered that day, almost 40 years ago?'

I reflected that my entire existence on this planet had been consumed with fighting; not just the physical military wars, but also my relationships, my schooling, my career and more to the point, the war with myself, my continuous internal battle. I heard a voice say, 'Stop fighting!' as I lay back on the mat and felt great comfort in the foetal position. The pressure and tension drained out of me; everything was serene. There was no more scrapping, just a sense of peace within me the likes of which I'd never felt before. I closed my eyes and died.

When I opened them, I saw Laura lying next to me, her angelic blue eyes staring deep into my soul. I looked at her, stroked her cheek and said, 'Everything is going to be okay. Come with me.' I wasn't in a physical body any more, I was in the spirit world, and I could hear *everything* – the leaves dropping to the forest floor – and the colours were incredibly vibrant. It was the after-life; I was connected to the Universe and it was beautiful. All because I had let go and surrendered. Since the age of ten when I'd fought back against the chimp, it had been imprinted on me never to surrender, and that was further reinforced in my time in the forces. But you must surrender to yourself to become the person you really are. Another word in my head was *become*. If you want to take ownership of a situation you have to *become* the situation, not be just an element of it, and certainly not the victim. Become the host, not the guest.

I felt like I was in Utopia after the out-of-body experience, and thinking the ceremony had now ended, I put my trainers on, went over to Todd, one of the organisers and said, 'I know what it's like, I've seen it, the afterlife.' Then I left, went to my room and lay on my bed. Philosophy was racing through my mind like ticker-tape on a TV news channel, phrases like: 'Sorry, doesn't give you an excuse to do it anyway' and 'Pain screams the loudest when it's dying.' So many people had expressed so much pain these last few nights. I looked back on my life and marvelled that I had survived so much shit. Even in my darkest hour I'd found a smile. That would be a fitting epitaph. I felt amazing, grateful to be alive.

Just then, Jessie, the American organiser from the Heroic Hearts Project, and Dave came back in the room. I was full of beans, 'Hey guys, how are you!?' Jessie seemed concerned, while Dave, who I'd never seen so lost and broken, looked at me and said, 'I'm never doing this again. War was nothing compared to what I've just been through. If it wasn't such a controlled environment tonight, I would have killed myself.'

'What happened?' I asked, and then he told me his story.

THE HALLS OF VALHALLA

Like myself, Nicko had experienced very little the first night as the ayahuasca dose was too weak; in fact he'd nodded off! But come the second night's ceremony with a double dose poised at his lips, he asked *la medecina* to help him find closure for the death of three friends killed by an IED (improvised explosive device) in Afghanistan. In real life this had never been granted and was part of the fuel of his anger.

In his trance, Nicko was walking the great halls of an ancient castle. With its mighty walls and vaulted ceiling, he knew instantly it was Valhalla, the resting place of dead warriors. One of his dead friends was there to meet him and showed him around. It felt so real, seeing his friend's room and wandering the corridors of the castle. In a room with a bar sat all his lost friends who had perished in battle, friends who he'd never had the chance to say goodbye to, to hug them and tell them how much he loved them. He felt so happy to be there.

Out of nowhere, a Taliban fighter appeared. In real-life Afghanistan at the age of 23, Dave had mistakenly shot and killed this man whom he had thought was fixing an IED into the ground. While it was deemed 'justified' by the rules of engagement, the man was innocent and there was no bomb. Dave had never forgotten this man, nor the distress his action had caused his family. And yet here was the Afghan in Valhalla, staring back at him, his eyes full of forgiveness. They shook hands and he embraced Dave. Then one by one Nicko went to each of his friends at the bar hugged them and said goodbye. Before he left them, another of his friends, Kevin, took him to a door and opened it. Sitting on the bed, his mother was weeping. Nicko tried to talk to her but she couldn't hear him. He then began to realise the terrible strain his anger and his attempts at suicide had had on his family.

The drawbridge to Valhalla was now closed and gone. As Dave woke up, one of the staff asked him how he was. He answered that now he had said his goodbyes, he no longer needed to feel angry at what had happened to them; every time he now thought of them, he would see them at the bar all together, happy and united. It was nothing but positive. The closure he had asked for had been granted. But his journey with ayahuasca was far from over.

THE DEVIL IS A BLACK FIGURE OF SMOKE

On the third evening, Dave had a triple dose. He asked the teacher plant to show him what he needed to live a positive life, and soon he started seeing patterns, everything red but for the black shadow he was following who kept looking back at him and laughing scornfully. Shirtless and shoeless, fires licking around him, Dave passed by the gates of Hell, the figure coiling with pitch smoke, its mouth and eye sockets even blacker. Hunched over and exhausted, Dave waited for someone to come and help him, but no one came. That was his first lesson ... the only person who could help him was himself – he was all on his own.

A few hours later into his vision and Dave was moving uncontrollably, thinking, 'If I keep fighting, I'm going to die.' In that darkened hell, his body went limp and he was flying through a tunnel of infernal flame at light-speed, his body pulsing with anger and pain, warming him with hatred, anger enveloping him in a sheet of fire. Nicko next found himself being presented with all the bad things he'd ever done but was forced to witness them from the other person's view, as if he was in their shoes. He felt everything they felt and realised how insensitive he had been, but at the time he'd had no idea of his behaviour. It was overwhelming, he hated himself for it.

It was now plain to him the dark figure was the Devil. When Dave looked down his hands were dripping red and he was standing over his dead wife and kids, slain at his feet. He had become a killer again. The Devil screamed with laughter as Nicko tried to revive them ... tried for hours. Hell wouldn't go away, he was still beside the shadowy figure, his outline indistinct and curling with tendrils of black smoke. The sense that there was no way out of there, that his death was coming, was unshakeable.

He knew that a part of him had to die and there was nothing he could do about it. Overcome with self-pity and helplessness he began to sob. In the midst of tears, he realised he had a choice; he could will himself to die at that very moment if he wished. A sense of inevitability, sadness and desolation washed over him, as Dave felt there were still so many good things he could do to help other people before he died.

And as he began to die, so did his mind-based identity. He found himself drawing away from the soldier he had once been, the ghost of which he'd been holding on to since coming to civvy street. He became disengaged with old concepts about himself and everything he'd been holding on to. And with that death came the rebirth of his true self, the re-emergence of the unconditioned, unlabelled, unbiased sparkle of consciousness that is prior to and beyond any judgement or category. That night the purge he went through was the worst yet, the healer drawing out the black toxicity from Nicko's body and spitting it in his bucket, my friend convulsing and vomiting so severely, he felt as if his body was being turned inside out.

LAST RETURN TO CHIMP COUNTRY

I spent quite a long time trying to calm Nicko and reassure him his family were fine, it was just part of the vision. But I was absorbing his trauma. He wanted to call them and check they were okay, but I managed to persuade him against it. Eventually, he fell asleep. Unless you have a way of offloading trauma you take it on. And that's exactly what happened. As I lay back down I went back into chimp country. Unlike last night's attack, when I'd surrendered to the ape and the sound and emotion were absent, tonight's trip to the circus was very real; I was screaming, broken, crying in panic.

I lay in my bed and the chimp was on top of me every time I closed my eyes. This was the authentic replay of the attack that I had buried all those decades ago. It was an emotionally visceral attack, more than a physical one. I'd told such a watered-down, anaemic version of the story, while the real version that dripped with gore, snapped bones and blood, had been buried by my brain for my own sanity. This was the one moment I had not fully surrendered to, and now it was time to face my deepest fear and unlock the emotional pain of that day. This time the emotional trauma played itself out in full Dolby surround sound. The teacher plant had clearly not finished with me until this point.

WHERE THE RIVER MEETS THE SEA

The next day, Nicko told me he didn't want to go through it again, and nor did I, but I reminded him we were here to face our demons. During our spiritual travels we had both died out of necessity in order for the trauma to die too and for us to move on with our lives. That final night Nicko took the teacher plant for the fourth time and it sent him back into the familiar wasteland of flame. He'd always felt diminished and without an identity since leaving the Special Forces, as if he was a weak, diluted version of his former self, but now he found himself arguing with the Devil, telling him, 'I control my mind, not you!' The shaman came over to him. Nicko sat up, listening as the female shaman sang, breathing slowly as if swallowing her song. When he opened his eyes it was his wife singing to him. Falling back into the trance, she was waiting for him. She held his hand and said, 'We'll do this together.' All the images of things he'd been through, losing his mates in Afghanistan, killing the man by accident, in fact, every-thing he'd kept away from her she was now witnessing. They were a team now, he knew he could trust her and had someone to fall back on.

In his own words: 'When I got back from Costa Rica, everyone back home said to me I was a different person, I was more approachable. Because I was at ease, people felt at ease with me. I never wanted to intimidate people. I feel at ease with myself now. I'm grateful for my life, my children and wife, my house, car. I feel like I've left my PTSD behind me. My wife said I used to violently jump around in my sleep, but now I sleep soundly and deeply. I have so much more energy and want to help others. I think I'm a better person. You've really got to want to change for the truth plant to work.'

My last night, I wanted to return to the afterlife as this place had felt amazing. But as I started to leave my body, floating away formlessly, I saw those that were close to me, Laura, my mum and family, with tears in their eyes as they tried their best to pull me back. It may be awesome but my work and life experience are far from finished. I belong here.

And my final night's journey was full of colour, love, gratitude and compassion. The chimp was gone, the tortured river of pain from so many summers past, once so dammed up and twisted inside my mind, had now reached the sea and with its course the ape that had fractured my psyche had now left as a friend.

A measure of mental health is the disposition to find good everywhere. When negative things happen, your opinion is the conduit for further suffering or positive outcomes, it's your choice. If you are waiting for something good to happen to change your view, it's likely you'll be waiting a long time. After any traumatic event it's natural to want to be the person you were before it all happened, but you're not that person any longer. The more you fight for what you're not, the less you'll accept who you newly are.

Accept, appreciate and surrender to yourself. Humans are spiritual beings living a physical experience. Everything is our choice. I now fully support that who I am shapes what I am! I am what I am, there is no façade, no mask and for that very fact I feel more like me than I've ever felt before.

EPILOGUE

As the plane touched down at Heathrow, Dave and I were whisked into a car bound for Bury St Edmunds. Christmas was just a few weeks away and it was the final venue of a short theatre tour I'd been on, talking about my life's experiences. Before my departure to Central America, the issue my team and I were concerned about was that I would have to be in the public eye so quickly after taking *la medecina* – what if it had negative effects? It could all end in disaster! There's nothing like standing under a spotlight in front of 500 people if you're going to screw up and lose your mind. So far, the tour had been amazing, we'd created a simulation, taking audience members as mock-hostages to make it as interactive as possible. But come the gig in Bury St Edmunds, despite the fact we'd been halfway round the world that day (and further still in the spirit realm), it was the best performance of the lot and we went out on a high. It wasn't just that the audience were appreciative, I felt *different*. Gone was the self-criticism, that annoying character trait of feeling I was being constantly judged. After a lifetime of friction living in the wrong skins, the restlessness and discomfort, I've finally removed the burden of self-doubt and found the inner me.

And Nicko? There's no doubt I saw Dave go through hell at Soltara, however, I also saw him pass through heaven on his fourth evening with Ayahuasca Airlines, and that is when he decided his life was worth living. Dave is a very different person to the one I left the UK with in Dec 2019; you can see it in his face, hear it in his words. He's committed to himself and his beautiful wife and children. I know in my heart he will be a better person not only for himself, but for all that are close and encounter him. He's now at peace with himself and has clarity, focus and happiness. I cannot thank the Heroic Hearts Project enough for their kindness, and also the guidance and professionalism of the staff at Soltara's amazing facility. One in five veterans returned from Afghanistan are said to suffer from PTSD, and Heroic Hearts are proving to the medical establishment that using psychedelic medicine in a safe, controlled environment is having great results in treating it. For myself and Nicko, the ayahuasca treatment was hugely effective. One of our 18 participants considered his week at Soltara equal in its impact to the two years of traditional treatment he'd already received. I was so moved by my own experience and the transformative effect ayahuasca had on Nicko, that I have now become a Heroic Hearts ambassador.

I proposed to Laura on New Year's Eve, 2019. I'm a very impulsive person, but I can tell you this was the most prolonged decision I've ever made. Jaded by our past experiences, marriage is something both myself and Laura have always been scornful of. To be honest, I'd been a little apprehensive that the whole Soltara experience might affect our relationship (or, more to the point, me), but the teacher plant gave me the clarity I needed, and while in Costa Rica, I decided to make a commitment. Laura has sacrificed so much for me and the businesses we run together while also bringing up her son, William. Up until now, I've never felt the pure essence of love from another as I do from her. I may have been loved in the past, but, due to my self-loathing I didn't feel I deserved it and built a wall around myself so it couldn't get in. Although I had doubts that Laura wanted to get married, I knew deep down at the least it would make her feel more secure for William and herself. If anything happened to me, my business projects would also be left to her, as she has been part of everything I have created from scratch.

It was almost midnight, when I asked her to join me next to the fire. Ever the planner, I'd pre-loaded the ring into a hiding spot close by where we were now sitting with our glasses of alcohol-free champagne. I told Laura I had just one more present for her. She giggled with excitement as I presented her with a small box, her eyes widening as she opened it and gasped, immediately shutting the lid! As breathless as I, she opened the box a second time and gazed at the diamond-studded ring in wonder. I found it hard to get my words out; it wasn't so much a question of, 'Will you marry me?' more about how I felt about her, and that I would always love and protect her and her son, and that I'd like to get married at *some* point, *if* she agreed we should. And luckily for me, she said yes! And that, my friends, is the end – for now.

Now is the time for your call for action. After you've read this, please go and set yourself a goal, a challenge that scares you a little. Tell everyone about it and make yourself accountable. After I returned from series two of SAS: *Who Dares Wins*, I contacted an organisation called 'One Year No Beer' as I was so pleased with my two months' sobriety and wanted to take it further. I wanted to make myself accountable. Like it or not we are susceptible to others' judgement, so you may as well make it work for you – tell people of your goal, let them know what you're aiming for and when. Because if you don't tell a soul, nobody will know if you've abandoned your challenge, and no one will hold you to account. We all have the capability within ourselves of doing extraordinary things, it's our choice. As we come to an end part of me wants to say to you, 'Good luck!', but you don't need it. Just follow the steps in this book and you'll get where you need to go. Be brave, be focused, be Battle Ready.

For more supporting material and for my fitness programmes please head to www.ollieollerton.co.uk

FURTHER READING

Books to inspire, provoke and further your journey.

Break Point
By Ollie Ollerton – My autobiography covers a whirlwind of events including my early days, as a juvenile delinquent, SAS Selection, taking fire from kidnappers in Iraq; busting child trafficking rings in Thailand and battling the demons of drink and depression in order to get my life back.

The Very Best of Friedrich Nietzsche: Quotes from a Great Thinker
By David Graham – stuffed full of the German philosopher's best quotes on life, suffering, self-knowledge and hope.

Recovery: Freedom From Our Addictions
By Russell Brand – Hard earned, searing wisdom from the comic wordsmith, following his journey in the 12-Step programme of Alcoholics Anonymous.

Make Your Bed: Small Things That Can Change Your Life... And Maybe The World
By retired US Navy Seal, Admiral William H. McRaven – This brilliant little book has wise pearls about growing good habits, teamwork, courage and pulling the best out of yourself.

Man's Search For Meaning
By Viktor E. Frankl – Based on Frankl's experience in the Nazi deathcamps, this book shows that even at our most dehumanized we can still possess humanity.

A New Earth
By Eckhart Tolle – Tolle shines a light on human dysfunction, self-ishness and the overactive ego, teaching us that real freedom is found by being in the now.

You Are the Placebo: Making Your Mind Matter
By Joe Dispenza – By using the right thoughts and behaviours we can heal ourselves of physical and mental illness and reconfigure our reality.

Stand Up Straight
By Major General Paul Nanson – Great tips from the famous Officer's Military Academy on taking pride in yourself and the way you go about things, establishing new habits and how to cope under stress.

In the Realm of Hungry Ghosts
By Doctor Gabor Maté – Maté spent 12 years working with addicts in Vancouver's skid row. Refreshing in its take on addiction.

The 5 Second Rule
By Mel Robbins – If you have an urge to fulfil a goal, unless you act on it within five seconds, your brain will kill it. Brilliant and inspirational.

Meditations
By Marcus Aurelius – Taken from the great Roman Emperor's diaries and notes to himself, this book is packed with quotes on self-control, justice, wisdom and courage; the four pillars of Stoicism.

Ten Arguments For Deleting Your Social Media Accounts Right Now
By Jaron Lanier – An ex-Silicon Valley scientist spills the beans on the mental health dangers of social networks.

ACKNOWLEDGEMENTS

Big thank you to David Riding at MBA, my editor Matt Phillips and his team at Blink who bring my creativity to the surface, and my ghost writer Richard Waters who simply understands everything I think and say. I commend you all.

Laura, you are amazing and I cannot thank you enough for your unconditional love and support and for keeping the business wheels firmly inflated and in constant motion even while I'm away.

Everyday I give gratitude to myself for the structure and discipline exercised to bring myself from what seemed like a bottomless pit of despair and depression. Six years ago I would have never believed where I am today even in my wildest of dreams. Never stop giving yourself credit for all you achieve.

To the reader: if you were hoping this book would provide a magic formula, understand that the magic is within you, I simply provide the stepping stones from my own experience that worked so well for me. I wrote this book for other people to see that there is a better way for us all to live a fuller happier life. If you are reading this section of the book there's a good chance you've read the content. Well done for investing in yourselves and I hope this serves as the catalyst to change for good.

To the incredible team at Soltara who open the gates to self-development, love and understanding.

Jesse at The Heroic Hearts Project, well done brother! Having the insight to discover an alternative method of recovery for our veterans deserves massive praise in advance for all that you help and, in some cases, save. I look forward to guiding veterans from the UK to you. Thank you to all the sponsors that make it possible to be treated through The Heroic Hearts Project.

I am so grateful for my amazing family, who are a massive part of my drive and passion to succeed, I love you all.

And last but not least, I have no idea what happened to you after that day but I think about you often and praise you for your actions, you showed selfless love to your baby and did what any species would do to protect its own. You have been a part of my life I don't regret and I hope you had a peaceful life away from the circus. Love you Chimp!

INDEX

OLLIE OLLERTON WILL RETURN

BIG NEWS COMING SUMMER 2020

GO TO
WWW.OLLIEOLLERTON.COM/PROJECT-X